Prayers
for
DIFFICULT
TIMES

Women's Edition

Prayers
for
DIFFICULT TIMES

❧

Women's Edition

EMILY BIGGERS

BARBOUR BOOKS
An Imprint of Barbour Publishing, Inc.

© 2016 by Barbour Publishing, Inc.

Print ISBN 978-1-63409-789-5

eBook Editions:
Adobe Digital Edition (.epub) 978-1-63409-982-0
Kindle and MobiPocket Edition (.prc) 978-1-63409-983-7

Published by Barbour Books, an imprint of Barbour Publishing, Inc., P.O. Box 719, Uhrichsville, Ohio 44683, www.barbourbooks.com

Our mission is to publish and distribute inspirational products offering exceptional value and biblical encouragement to the masses.

Member of the
Evangelical Christian
Publishers Association

Printed in the United States of America.

Contents

Introduction

Give all your worries and cares to God, for he cares about you.
1 PETER 5:7 NLT

Women are verbal creatures. It's been said that the average woman uses approximately 13,000 more words than the average man in a day. When this statistic is quoted, we women laugh because most of us cannot deny that we like to talk! We often find ourselves seeking answers and strength from other people.

When you face a trial, do you find that you're tempted to call or text a friend before you take the concern to God? Do you rely on your husband, mother, or sister too heavily at times?

This book provides you with some prayer starters that will help you take your troubles straight to your heavenly Father. He longs to be the One you turn to in your times of deep need. We are daughters of a sovereign God. He always hears our prayers. He chooses to answer prayers in different ways. He may calm the raging storm around you, or He may bring a peace over you as He carries you through the storm. Use these prayer starters to help you begin conversations with God. He is ready and able to help you in the most difficult of circumstances.

Abuse

*This means that anyone who belongs to Christ has become
a new person. The old life is gone; a new life has begun!*
2 CORINTHIANS 5:17 NLT

*I*f you are experiencing—or have experienced—
any type of abuse, you know the pain it inflicts.
Whether the abuse is physical or verbal, it's
wrong and it's not your fault. God created all
men and women equally, and He sees us through
a "Jesus lens." When He looks at you, He sees
a righteous daughter. You have been made
spotless by your Savior's death upon the cross.
When you accepted Him, He forgave you of sin
and a new life began in you.

Don't allow anyone to purposefully bring
harm to you. While it is certainly God's will
for you to "turn the other cheek," this does
not mean to tolerate abuse. You must seek help
immediately if you are in danger of any kind.

Lord, You saw Paul when You looked at Saul. You bring beauty from ashes. Sometimes I wonder how You could love me. I don't even love myself at times. Help me this day to see the lies others have told me about myself as what they are—lies. Remind me of the truth that I am fearfully and wonderfully made in Your image and that You have great plans for my future.

Jesus, I feel alone at times when I think about what has been done to me. I wonder if it's somehow my fault. Thank You for reassuring me time after time that it's not my fault and that You are here with me even in my darkest hour. Help me to sense Your presence now, I pray. You are my Savior, and You have promised to never leave me. What a wonderful promise!

God, I'm afraid when I see a certain person or type of person. I feel the fear wash over me again. I keep thinking I've put the memories behind me, but then there they are again. I feel the sting of abuse as fresh as the times when it occurred. Please take control of my thoughts and cast out Satan and his desire to pull me down.

Heavenly Father, I look back and I see the pain but also Your provision. I see the way You took me out of yesterday and brought me into today, Father. In the Bible, Your people built altars as reminders. I call to mind in this moment the ways in which You have rescued me. I thank You for the people who have helped me. I read in Your Word of Your great love for me. Continue to heal my heart, I pray, in ways that only You can.

As a woman, Father, I feel so vulnerable. I fear being hurt again. I know that I can't hide behind walls. Help me to trust You, Lord, and give me wisdom about the people I can trust. Show me safe people, God.

I love the verse in scripture that says the battle is the Lord's. My battle is not with weapons or against a large army, but it feels every bit as challenging! I fight a battle to love myself and to forgive the ones who have hurt me. I fight it every day. I'm thankful that the battle is Yours, Jesus. I can't do it on my own.

I am Yours, and that's enough today, Jesus. I belong to the Messiah, the Savior of the world. This world has its troubles, but I know that with You in my heart, I can survive. We've got this!

Accidents

And we know that in all things God works for the good of those who love him, who have been called according to his purpose.
ROMANS 8:28 NIV

A wise woman told her family, "While we have received many blessings, we are not immune to the troubles of this world." Within weeks, there was a tragic accident in her own family. The woman and her loved ones grieved the loss of a child taken from them at a young age.

It was impossible to feel this could be the will of God, and yet the woman remembered a scripture that said all of our days are numbered and that God ordained each one of them before we were born. Had God looked away and forgotten this family? Had He gone to sleep on the job and allowed this tragedy? Certainly not!

This is a fallen world we live in, and accidents happen. But good can come even from the worst of situations and the deepest losses. For now, we only see in part, but one day we will be granted full understanding. Trust Him. God is always in control, even when accidents take place.

Father, I know that there is a time for everything. Your Word tells me this. I don't understand how this could be part of Your plan, but I pray You will use even this for Your glory. May I look back one day in the future and see how Your hand was at work in my life even though it was a very difficult time.

God, I know that You are in control. Just as You care for the sparrows and the lilies of the field, You take care of my needs. I am Your daughter. You will never take Your hand off my life.

I sometimes feel the shock I experienced after the accident. It seems like I'm living it again. Instead of shock, envelop me in peace, stability, and calm. You brought me through, and You will continue to do so. . .day by day.

God, in Your Word it seems like You are always turning bad things into good things. You struck down Saul on the road to Damascus only to raise him up as a great leader. You brought a flood, but when it was over, You made the world into a better place. Use this accident. Use this pain. Create a new thing here, and cause me to see and appreciate it.

I wake up in the night, Father, troubled and scared. I'm so impacted by this tragedy, and I feel like I will never be the same. Remind me that I can lie down and rest peacefully because You are watching over me. I ask this in the powerful name of Jesus who heals.

You did not look away or forget us, God. You were there. Help me to trust that Your ways are higher than mine and Your thoughts are higher than my thoughts.

God, these are hard days. I wake up to the sun shining through my window, and I wonder how it could be so bright and pretty outside when I feel so sad and sick inside. I know that it may take time, but I pray that You will restore in my heart a sense of joy. And for today, Lord, will You carry me? Will You please remind me that You are so very close and that You have not—and will not *ever*—let me go?

Dear Lord, You are omnipotent and omnipresent. You always have my best in mind. And in You there are no "accidents."

This just wasn't how I wanted things to go, Father. I can't believe this actually happened and that I'm sitting here in the midst of what seems impossible to overcome. Give me strength to face the mountains ahead, because in You, all things are possible. Even healing. Even moving forward from this hardship.

Addiction

*"Be careful, or your hearts will be weighed down
with carousing, drunkenness and the anxieties of life,
and that day will close on you suddenly like a trap."*
LUKE 21:34 NIV

*N*o one plans to become an addict. No one
turns on the pornographic movie or takes the
drink or pops the painkiller with the realization
or goal that she is stepping onto a road to
destruction. And yet, families are destroyed, jobs
lost, and hearts trapped every day by addictions.

As human beings, we naturally look for
something to fill the gaps in our lives, the empty
spots, the lonely moments, the disappointments.
When we fill those gaps with anything but Jesus,
we come up empty-handed again and again. We
go back for one more drink, one more pill, one
more. . .whatever the addiction may be.

Nothing has the power to fill the God-spot
in your heart besides God Himself. *Nothing.* Turn
and run from that which has a hold of your life.
It's nothing but a trap keeping you from the
abundant life Jesus offers.

Each day is a new start. Help me this day to resist the temptation to take an easier way out. Help me to stay the course. God, my addiction causes me nothing but sickness and grief. Remind me that Your ways are pure and good and that they always bring me out on top.

Father, I can't do this on my own. Please place in my path just the right counselor, group, or program. I pray that You will guide my steps and give me the strength to keep walking in the right direction.

I am a new creation in You, Jesus. I thought that would mean that I'm no longer tempted. I thought I would wake up a changed woman and ready to face life addiction-free, but I'm still struggling. Walk with me. Show me the way. Help me to trust Your timing as You heal me and set me free.

I wish that I could wave a magic wand and cause the one I love to walk away from this addiction. I feel like I have to compete with it day and night. I can't change the situation, but I can bring it to You in prayer. I put this whole thing into Your strong and capable hands, heavenly Father. I ask that You change what I cannot.

Jesus, I carry a cross every day. It is a sick addiction that brings me nothing good. It offers nothing beneficial to anyone in my life. It only brings pain, pain, and more pain. I will carry this cross. I will seek to be entirely free of it one day, but if it's always there in the back of my mind, let it be a thing of the past and not something that continues to destroy my present and my future.

I remember a line from the children's song "Jesus Loves Me" that says "I am weak and He is strong." That rings so true today. I thought I could beat this thing anytime I wanted—all by myself. I was so wrong. I need You, Lord, to help me stay sober. I need You every minute of every day. I am weak, but hallelujah—You are strong!

Help me, Lord, to look deep into my heart and examine my ways. Show me where I hurt those I love—my parents, my husband, my children, my friends. Help me to take an honest inventory of my life. I want to change. I need Your help.

Help me to surrender and lay my addiction down at Your feet, Father. I have to keep starting over. I feel like a failure. Be the lifter of my head. Be my defender against the enemy who wants to keep me captive in this addiction.

Adultery

Would you welcome a stray dog into your home to destroy things? If he stood at the door of your house showing his ugly teeth, would you beckon to him, "Come on in, boy! Go for it!" Of course not! We laugh at such a suggestion. And yet, every day, women allow dangerous enemies into their marriages. It may start as simple as flirtation. It may feel good to receive a compliment from a man you work with or see at the grocery store. Your own husband may have been preoccupied lately or a bit inattentive. . .and here is someone who notices your beauty or your worth. Be wary. Adultery does not begin in the bedroom. Jesus warned against even a glance at another man. Honor God by honoring your husband.

God, he wasn't faithful, but he says he wants to be now. I don't know how to respond. Give me wisdom. Grant me the ability to face these decisions and difficulties which seem so insurmountable to me. I never dreamed I would end up here. I'm glad You have not left me, even now.

I was unfaithful. How could I have done these things and been untrue to my husband? I feel like I've committed the unforgivable sin. Yet You tell me in Your Word You can forgive any sin through the blood of Jesus shed on the cross. I know the words, but I pray You will help them reach deep into my heart where I can somehow forgive myself. I don't like who I've become, and I pray for supernatural change in my life that can only come about through Your grace and forgiveness.

Lord, I blame him. Every day I wake up blaming him. The blame is starting to eat at me and build a fortress of bitterness in my very spirit. It's affecting everything I do. . .every word I speak. It's dragging me down to a low, low place. Remove the blame from my heart. Remind me that I am far from perfect and that it's not all his fault. Show me areas where I need to change, and soften my heart where it needs to be softened, I ask in Your name.

Help me, Jesus, to lay this burden down at Your feet. I read about how You called upon those men gathered around the adulterous woman to throw the first stone if they were without sin. I am not without sin. Forgive me, Father, and help me to forgive.

Sweet Jesus, I am broken. Where once there was trust, there is distrust. Where once there was intimacy, I feel stone cold. Show me the way forward. Make it clear, I pray. I need You now like never before. I can't get through this on my own.

Dear heavenly Father, You were there. You saw my unfaithfulness. Let's call it what it was. Adultery. You know my sin, and yet You love me still. Tears stream down my face. My heart hurts so deeply with something I can never take back. Help me to never make this mistake again.

I know the voice of my Shepherd. I have been listening to it for many years. I am being called upon in a way I never knew possible to tune into that voice and seek direction only from the One who knows me best. Give me grace for the moment and the healing and power to get through this, Lord.

Alcohol Abuse

*The Spirit and the bride say, "Come!" And let the one
who hears say, "Come!" Let the one who is thirsty come;
and let the one who wishes take the free gift of the water of life.*
REVELATION 22:17 NIV

*A*lcohol is merely a substance, a liquid that is
contained in a bottle; and yet when unleashed,
it has great power and can wreak havoc in a life.
Alcoholism destroys marriages, families, and
futures.

Know that there is a fulfillment for your
thirst. There is an escape from the life you've
fallen into—a life that relies on survival until you
can get that next drink. There is living water.
There is Jesus.

You may be so addicted and drawn to
alcohol that you feel powerless over it. That's a
great beginning—recognizing that you are not
strong enough to overcome this on your own,
recognizing the need for help. As you step out
in faith and seek help through an addiction
recovery program, God will give you the strength
you need day by day. Trade the substance of
sickness for living water, and you will never
thirst again.

Help me this day, Father, to be wise rather than foolish. Help me to refrain from drinking, which leads me to do things that are not pleasing to You. Help me instead to be filled with Your Holy Spirit. Give me the ability to see all that You have done for me and to be thankful. I'm thankful in advance for the way I believe You are going to save me from alcoholism (Ephesians 5:17–20).

It's not easy to admit that I have a problem with alcohol, God. I'm such an in-control person. I go to work. I manage my household. I am a good person overall. Where did this addiction come from, and why does it have such a hold on me? I pray for the ability to see it for what it is today, Lord. A problem. Admitting it is the first step.

God, I want to be a woman of character and integrity, not someone who sneaks around finding my next drink. I want my life to be pleasing to You, and I want to be ready when You come back to take me home (Romans 13:13). I want You to find me living an honorable life. Help me to return to that, Father. Rescue me, I pray.

Lord, as a woman, I so loathe admitting weakness. But I admit that I'm abusing alcohol. I'm using it as a crutch. It has a grasp on my life like nothing else. I would trade my best friend or my last dollar for it. I have made it—although I never meant to—my god. It's such a pitiful god. It offers me nothing. Please intervene in this drama I have created for myself. Draw me back to a place of safety where pleasant borders are established in my life. I love You, Lord (Psalm 16:6).

Father, You healed the blind and the lame and even those with leprosy. I know that You can heal me, too. I didn't see myself as sick for a long time, but now I am beginning to. This is an illness. I need Your divine intervention. I need You to show up as the Great Physician in my life.

Lord, it's so hard to be different. Other people can have just one drink. I can't stop with that. I wish I could. I hate being this way. Please provide for me just the right helpers, people who are like me, people who have escaped this prison and have begun a new life free from alcohol.

Anger

*When you are angry, do not sin, and be sure
to stop being angry before the end of the day.*
EPHESIANS 4:26 NCV

*A*nger is a normal emotion. We all feel it from
time to time. It's not anger itself that causes the
trouble, but rather, our reaction to our angry
feelings. Our reactions often involve words and
even actions that are not pleasing to God.

Have you reacted in anger toward your
husband or children? Your coworkers or boss?
Friends and relatives? Think about what you
would do differently if you were granted a "do-
over." Would you stop and take a deep breath?
Could you step away and allow yourself some
time to calm down before lashing out?

Like toothpaste squeezed from a tube is
impossible to put back in, so are angry words
impossible to take back once they're spoken.

To be a godly woman, you must allow God to
help you with anger. Begin by asking Him today.

Dear God, I know that anger lives in pain. Where there is hurt in my life, I often react in anger. Things I regret later explode from my mouth. Please heal the pain in me and set a guard over my tongue so that I will not hurt others in my anger.

Jesus, when You got angry, it was a righteous anger. I get angry when things don't go my way or when others say or do things to hurt me. Help me not to be so egocentric. Help me to be kingdom-centered.

Lord, James 1:19–20 sums it up. I want to be quick to listen to what others have to say; slow to speak; and even slower to lose my temper. My anger will never produce Your righteousness in my life. Please help me to take Your Word into my heart and allow it to transform me.

Remind me, God, that You are the giver of all good gifts. You don't withhold any good gift from Your children whom You love. Sometimes I feel like You're not giving me what I want or need. I grow angry with You even though I feel terribly guilty about that anger. Please forgive me and show me how to trust You even when I'm not getting my way.

God, I often lose control and act in ways that I wish I didn't. It keeps happening. Please guard my heart and my tongue. . .and please, Lord, help me to have self-control. I long to be more like Jesus.

Help me not to sin in my anger, Father. Everyone feels angry sometimes. I never want to act on it. Help me to take a deep breath and first come to You in prayer. Rescue me from my own anger, I pray.

Heavenly Father, I sometimes hurt my husband and children when I'm angry. I hurt them with my words. I say things that I know are unkind, and later, I feel so guilty for it. Reveal to me where this anger comes from, God. Show me the hurt within my heart that reacts with a hot temper. Root out the bitterness in me. I am ready to get to work. I want this to change.

God, You want Your children to live at peace with one another. You tell us never to let the sun go down on our anger. I find myself stewing about a situation when I go to sleep and then picking right up where I left off the next day as soon as I wake. I know this is not Your will for me. Help me to value my relationships more and to resolve conflicts quickly.

Anxiety

Do not worry about anything, but pray and ask
God for everything you need, always giving thanks.
PHILIPPIANS 4:6 NCV

Anxiety disguises itself. It may appear as a twitch or a pain. It causes headaches. It's a tightness in the chest or an uncontrollable shakiness in the legs. It is a fear that's unnecessary and yet, like a puppy freed from its leash, anxiety is impossible to control once it takes over your mind.

We are commanded in scripture to trade worry for prayer. Start today. Every time an unwanted thought intrudes, block it with a prayer. Even speaking the name of Jesus in such moments has great power. Jesus does not want you to be weighed down and burdened by worry. He asks you to release your cares to Him and let Him take care of you. Day by day, hour by hour, even moment by moment, learn to trust Him more. He will always come through, and in the end, you will see that the worry did not change things—but the prayers did!

Lord, I'm a worrier. I worry about my family and my friends. I worry about the future because there are so many unknowns. I know that in my anxiety I sin because I'm not trusting You. Please replace my fear with faith. Please help me to rely on You when I begin to worry needlessly.

When I'm anxious, I pray that You will remind me that I must cast my cares on You, Jesus. You ask me to do this. You tell me to cast them. That means rid myself of them. That means throw them with all my might at Your feet. Help me to truly surrender to You, Lord.

God, no one knows the secret fears that I carry around in my heart. No one but You. May I lay down fear and pick up confidence instead. You are my confidence and my peace.

I know, Lord Jesus, that I must trust You with my children. I feel so responsible for them! They are young and vulnerable. They may make the wrong choices. Help me to trust You with my most precious gifts. You made them and know them far better than even I do. Be with them, Lord, and watch over them. Cause me to trust that You have them in Your care.

God, this anxiety is wearing me down. It's a spiritual battle, but it's even taking a physical toll on me. I can't sleep or eat properly. I'm exhausted. Heal my mind and heart. Take away the fear and the panic. Replace them with peace and calm. I long to rest in You. I know that I can't do it on my own. I need You to help me get there, God.

Anxiety is like a prison that I cannot break free from no matter how hard I try. I need help, God. It is so hard to admit that. Give me wisdom this day about how to get help. Strip away my pride. I pray You will provide the help I so desperately need and that I will not be too prideful to accept it.

You are a good, good Father, and I am loved by You. When I'm afraid of others or of circumstances, remind me of Your goodness. When I feel I cannot face the future, remind me that I am Your beloved daughter. You are always good, and I am always loved. I am going to be just fine.

God, I notice that when I pray regularly, my anxiety decreases. I trust in You. Strengthen my prayer life that I might be freed from these anxious thoughts.

Arguments

*Again I say, don't get involved in foolish, ignorant
arguments that only start fights. A servant of the
Lord must not quarrel but must be kind to everyone.*
2 TIMOTHY 2:23–24 NLT

*R*emember junior high? Even high school?
Girls could be so catty. There was always drama
going on in the halls, and it penetrated the
classes and extracurricular activities as well.
It almost seemed as if some girls were picking
fights on purpose.

We look back and shake our heads at some of
the things that caused arguments—boys, grades,
even someone copying a hairstyle. And yet. . .are
things really all that different in our grown-up
world?

What can you "let go" today? What argument
can you avoid simply by holding your tongue?
Could your roommate or friend use a dose
of grace? Could you give up that opportunity
to defend your opinion with your husband or
friend? Refuse to get involved in petty fights. It
is dishonoring to your God.

God, Your Word emphasizes love over and over again. In I Corinthians, we read that it's even greater than hope and peace. Please help me to show love to others. I don't want to have an argumentative spirit. Please help me to be kind and loving at all times, even when things don't go my way.

Remind me, Father, that I may be the only Jesus some will ever see. Please help me to be a loving example of what it means to be a Christian. I see Christians arguing the cause of Christ in such an angry, bitter manner. I don't believe this is how You want us to do it. In fact, I know it isn't.

When I am tempted to argue, remind me to remain silent. There is a time for everything (Ecclesiastes 3), including a time to speak and a time to be quiet.

Lord, I know that the tongue can be a positive or a negative. Help me to use my words to bring You honor and glory rather than cause petty arguments. You take no pleasure in hearing Your children squabble with one another over issues that really don't matter in the long run. Help me to be more like Jesus. Help me to be slow to anger.

I want to bear fruit for You in this world, Father. I know that without spending time in prayer daily, I lose sight of my purpose on earth. I'm to bring glory to You and to lead others to know You as their personal Savior. How can I do this if I'm constantly at odds with those around me? Help me to love those whom You have placed in my circles of influence. I want to be known as a peacemaker.

Proverbs warns against stirring up anger. It says that this will bring nothing but trouble. Please help me to have the strength to walk away from arguments, Lord. I'm imperfect, and I will fail at this sometimes. Give me the wisdom and patience to deal with the outcome. Give me the humility to be the first to apologize and to make amends.

I know that You don't want me to covet what others have (Exodus 20:17). Jealousy stirs up anger and arguing among even Christian brothers and sisters. Help me to celebrate with others when good things come to them rather than grow jealous or bitter toward them. I want my heart to be right before You and before men.

Betrayal

It is not an enemy who taunts me—I could bear that.
It is not my foes who so arrogantly insult me—I could
have hidden from them. Instead, it is you—my equal,
my companion and close friend. What good fellowship we
once enjoyed as we walked together to the house of God.
PSALM 55:12–14 NLT

*J*ust before He was crucified, Jesus shared what
has come to be known as the Last Supper with
His disciples. These were the twelve with whom
He had walked closely. This was His inner circle.
And yet, one of these men betrayed Him, selling
information about His whereabouts for a mere
thirty pieces of silver. Wasn't He worth more to
Judas than material wealth?

Jesus understands the sting of betrayal. He
knows about the one who appears to be a friend
but isn't. He gets it.

As Christ did, so must we do. If we claim to
be Christians, we must forgive and respond in
love even when we are betrayed.

Heavenly Father, I feel so deeply hurt. I trusted him. He betrayed me. I know You tell me to guard my heart for it is the wellspring from which life flows. I didn't. I let my heart go too easily. I put it in the hands of another. In doing so, I was unfaithful to You, Lord. Hold me close. It hurts to find out that he's not the man I believed him to be.

Lord, it hurts to have a fickle friend. Even small betrayals leave wounds. I make plans with this friend, and she continues to break them at the last minute. She doesn't show up. She calls to cancel. Please guide me as to whether I should continue to show grace or perhaps back away a bit from this person. I need friends whom I can count on to be there.

Lord, I betrayed my friend. I shared information that was not to be shared. I have not been trustworthy. Whether my friend knows or not doesn't matter. I feel so guilty inside. Please forgive me for being a gossip. In the moment, it feels good to be the one in the know. Afterward, it saddens me that I was not true to my friend. *"A gossip betrays a confidence, but a trustworthy person keeps a secret"* (Proverbs 11:13 NIV).

None of the disciples wanted to believe that he could be the one who would betray You. And yet, in reality, it could have been any of them— just as it could be me. We are all sinners. We fall short. We mess up. Judas betrayed You, Jesus. It hurts me to read the story. Please keep my heart true to You, no matter the cost, all the days of my life.

I sit here hurting in disbelief. Betrayal stings. You know the sting of betrayal. You were betrayed by Peter three times before the cock crowed. He said he would never turn away from You and yet, it happened. Remind me that in our humanity we are weak. Give me a forgiving spirit that I might reach a place where I can forgive those who have betrayed me.

God, it seems like marriage is a thing of the past. I watch my friends' marriages disintegrating. Husbands are betraying wives, and wives are betraying husbands. Help me to remain true to my wedding vows and loyal to my mate.

Lord, I can't believe that someone would turn on me like this—all for the sake of climbing the ladder or getting the credit! Please use this to teach me how it feels to be betrayed that I might never treat others in such a manner.

Bitterness

Get rid of all bitterness, rage and anger, brawling and slander,
along with every form of malice. Be kind and compassionate to one
another, forgiving each other, just as in Christ God forgave you.
EPHESIANS 4:31–32 NIV

Any good gardener knows that it's just as important to get the weeds out as it is to plant the seeds. Certainly nothing healthy or beautiful can grow in a garden full of weeds. Bitterness, anger, and gossip are a lot like weeds. They start small, but soon, if they are not watched closely, they completely take over. Just as you wouldn't allow weeds to steal the nutrients of your garden's soil and suffocate new life, be on guard against this happening in your heart.

When you sense a hint of bitterness, trample it out. Ask God to pluck it from your heart so that it doesn't have the opportunity to gain control. Think about the grace that Jesus has shown to you and determine in your heart to demonstrate grace to those around you, even those who may receive unfair advantages or who may have hurt you in some way. Replace bitterness with kindness and forgiveness. This is God's will for you in Christ Jesus.

Lord, it's hard not to compare others' lives with my own. I see another woman's nice things. I'm envious of her husband who seems to be more caring than my own. I watch her children succeeding in areas where my own are struggling. Remind me that it's not good to compare myself to others. Help me to have a thankful and content heart that is right before You.

God, You name some things in Your Word that I should not allow to be part of my life. You tell me, in fact, to "get rid of" them. Bitterness is on Your list. Like an earthly father who does not allow his child to consume spoiled food because it will make her sick, You warn me against bitterness. You know it has the potential to ruin my life.

Lord, I'm bitter about a situation. You know all the players and the plot of the story. You know the details before I even spill them out before You. Please calm my spirit and give me the ability to let it go. I'm hurting myself more than anyone else when I hold on to this and stew about it day and night.

Jesus, someone did me wrong. You saw it. You were there. Why shouldn't I hold a grudge? I've been hurt and mistreated. You understand, You say? You, too, were wronged. You were treated unjustly. Your heart did not grow hard even when the soldiers put bitter vinegar to Your parched lips as You hung dying on the cross. You asked the Father to forgive them. Grant me just a tiny bit of that strength, Savior, that I might forgive those who have acted unfairly toward me.

Heavenly Father, I know that bitterness can take root and grow like a wild ivy, spreading through my very being. Please help me to be aware of its presence and root it out quickly.

Help me to focus on blessings over betrayals and friends over foes. Lord, I thank You for the people in my life, the opportunities You have given me, and the needs You meet every single day. I will choose to focus on the good rather than allow bitterness to fester in my heart.

One day at a time, Lord. Help me to forgive and forget and to simply take one day at a time. Help me to remember that nothing touches my life if it has not first been filtered through Your fingers. If You have allowed me to walk through a trial, there is a reason for it. Please keep me from becoming bitter toward You, my loving and faithful God.

Challenges

*When you go to war against your enemies and see horses
and chariots and an army greater than yours, do not be
afraid of them, because the LORD your God, who brought
you up out of Egypt, will be with you. When you are about
to go into battle, the priest shall come forward and address
the army. He shall say: "Hear, Israel: Today you are going
into battle against your enemies. Do not be fainthearted or
afraid; do not panic or be terrified by them. For the LORD
your God is the one who goes with you to fight for you
against your enemies to give you victory."*
DEUTERONOMY 20:1–4 NIV

There's a children's song that goes like this:
"My God is so big, so strong and so mighty!
There's nothing my God cannot do!"

It's easy to sing along with the kids and do
the fun hand motions, flexing our muscles
and pointing to the heavens to show that our
God is strong. But what about when you face
a challenge? When you get up each morning,
you know that there will be challenges in your
day—some days they are small, other days they
are giant!

Every single day you are going into battle and God goes with you. Before you put your feet on the floor, while you are still under the covers with your head resting on your pillow, commit your day to Him. Ask that He go with you and fight your battles for you. There is no challenge too great for our God.

Just as Noah built an ark and gathered pairs of animals when there was not a rain cloud in sight, I will face this day in complete faith that You are who You say You are. You are the God of the universe, and You are on my side. Help me know what to do regarding this obstacle that's in my way.

I think about young David with his slingshot. He was able to kill the giant not because of his own strength or expertise but because his confidence was in You, God. He was fighting the right battle. He was on the right side. Draw me close to You. I don't want to be on the front lines in this battle without You at my side as my commanding officer.

I remember learning in school that the brain must experience challenge or it will stop growing new dendrites. I suppose the spiritual life is like this as well. I tend to grow closer to You during times of trials. When life is just moving along normally, I often drift from You. When I face a challenge, I run to Your side. I'm more faithful in prayer. I seek You in Your Word, and I walk closer to Your side. Challenges can really be a positive thing in my life!

God, I'm struggling as a Christian woman in a very worldly society. I feel like others don't understand why I make the choices I make. It's hard being different. Your Word promises that the more I participate in the sufferings of Christ, the greater joy I will experience one day when His glory is fully revealed (1 Peter 4:13). Give me the endurance I need to stand firm in my faith.

Heavenly Father, the challenges I face are not unique to me. There's nothing strange about facing trials and hardships. Believers have walked through rough situations for generations. I should not be shocked when a challenge comes my way (1 Peter 4:12). Just as You have stood with Christ followers of the past, stand with me now, I pray. Walk with me, Lord. Carry me. I need Your help.

"Joshua fought the battle of Jericho, and the walls came tumbling down." I remember singing the song as a child, Lord. I was so surprised that when the men blew the trumpets and broke the pitchers, they were successful. Who would have ever thought? I could use some walls to come tumbling down about now, God. Show me the way. Make me open to unorthodox methods. I will tackle this challenge in any way You lead me, and then I will be able to stand back and watch You work. Thank You in advance for the guidance I know You will provide.

Chronic Illness

Have mercy on me, O LORD, for I am weak;
O LORD, heal me, for my bones are troubled.
PSALM 6:2 NKJV

*T*he occasional cold or flu can really get us down. But when illness becomes chronic, it can be so depressing. When you don't feel well for months, or even years on end, you may feel like just giving up.

Remember that God has not left you. Look for His provision even in this situation—doctors and nurses, medications, small comforts sent through family or friends. He has not left you.

It's natural to feel discouraged. Share those feelings with God. Look for ways that you can help others, for often, in doing so, you may feel better yourself. There may be something you can do, even in your condition, to help someone else.

In your illness, you are forced to trade a busy pace for a slower one. Use that time to pray for missionaries, others who are sick, and your own family and friends. Turn misery into a ministry! I know that You will bring healing either in this life or when I enter heaven one day, Lord. I will praise You even in my illness. Redeem my life from destruction. Crown me with Your loving-kindness and tender mercies (Psalm 103:1–4).

Father, I need You to walk with me day by day. I'm so tired of being sick. It keeps me from doing the things I long to do. I used to think nothing of running here and there. I wanted my life to slow down. Now I long to be busy again. Show me in some way today that I am not forgotten. I love You, God.

Jesus, You healed the sick. You caused the lame to walk. You took away the lepers' spots. I don't understand why You won't heal me in the same way. I know that there are things we just won't understand until we get to heaven. Please comfort me as I wait to understand Your ways.

Heavenly Father, this illness has begun to define me. I want my identity to be in Jesus Christ and not in my sickness. Please remind me that I am a cherished daughter of the King, saved by grace through faith in the Messiah. I'm not just a homebound sick person. I will not let Satan convince me that I'm just a burden and that others would be better off if I were not here. I have value and worth because I am part of the family of God.

Just as the apostle Paul prayed for You to remove the thorn from his flesh, I pray for this thorn to be taken from my life. I wait in expectation of what You will do. You will either remove it or You will continue to walk with me through this adversity, using it to strengthen my faith. I trust You, Lord, to do what is best for me.

Today I pray that each time I begin to dwell on what I *can't* do, Lord, You will bring to mind something that I *can*. I'm still able to do many things even though I'm ill. I can pray. I can encourage someone over the phone. I can do some things even though I'm not able to leave my home. Replace my negative thoughts with hopeful, positive ones. I can. I can. I can.

Chronic Pain

After you have suffered a little while, he will restore,
support, and strengthen you, and he will
place you on a firm foundation.
1 Peter 5:10 nlt

A little pain now and then is normal. Everyone experiences it. But chronic, unrelenting pain is quite another matter. To wake up in pain and endure it throughout each day, to go to bed with pain and start all over again the following day. . . It's not easy. It's taxing and draining to the body and eventually, to the spirit.

The good news is that God is with you always. Refuse to waste time trying to understand why He doesn't remove the pain. Tragedies and illnesses occur every day. We live in a fallen world where there is sorrow and disease. Your pain may diminish on this side of heaven and if not, you know that you are promised a new and perfect body in Paradise.

God is near. He promises to restore, support, and strengthen us, so that even in the midst of pain, we will stand on a firm foundation.

Jesus, You were fully man even as You were fully God. You came to earth and lived life as one of us. I can turn to You even when no one else is around, even when no one understands. You experienced great pain. You hung on the cross and gave Your very life for me. You died a painful death. Thank You for being my Savior and Friend. Thank You for being there for me every day and for walking with me through this pain.

God, I pray that You will give me wisdom and discernment as I seek new ways to control this pain. I thank You for medical professionals and others who assist me, and I pray that You will guide them as they treat my pain. At times the illness and discomfort get the best of me. I need You to be in control and to help me, Father.

I know that You never miss a tear that falls down my face, Lord. You gather my tears. You hear my cries for relief. One day there will be no more tears. One day I will run and dance and enjoy a new, flawless body. I will spend eternity in heaven with You. For now, remind me that You are near. Touch my weary brow. Restore my hope, I pray.

God, thank You that You are loving and slow to anger. Even when I grow angry with You for not healing me, You remain faithful to me until the anger takes its course and is replaced with a renewed hope and a rejuvenated faith. I'm sorry for being angry. I know that You are a good Father and that I am deeply loved by You.

Christ Jesus, You suffered greatly. I am not alone in this suffering. Enduring this pain is a way I can partake in Your sufferings. When Your glory is revealed to me, I will also share in Your gladness and joy (1 Peter 4:13).

Jesus, the apostle Paul tells me to rejoice in suffering. I must believe that somehow this suffering will produce endurance. . .and endurance will produce strength of character. . . and that hope will grow from that, a hope that will never be disappointed. Thank You for filling me with Your Holy Spirit (Romans 5:3–5).

God, I cast this burden of deep pain on You. I ask You to sustain me. I need You, Father, like never before (Psalm 55:22).

Church Discord

*There are six things the LORD hates—no, seven things he detests:
haughty eyes, a lying tongue, hands that kill the innocent, a
heart that plots evil, feet that race to do wrong, a false witness
who pours out lies, a person who sows discord in a family.*
PROVERBS 6:16–19 NLT

*C*hurch is supposed to be a safe place, God.
You may have found it to be just like the
world in some ways, and this can bring about
disillusionment and disappointment. The
politics and favoritism that occur at times
within the walls of the church don't go along
with the principles of God's Word. When you
experience hurt due to church discord, resist the
temptation to withdraw and point your finger,
calling those around you in the fellowship
"hypocrites." No good comes from that. God
desires that you be part of the solution rather
than a contributor to the problem. Ask Him
to clearly show you ways that you can make a
difference. All churches need to grow in this
area. As believers, we need to remember that we
are the family of God, the body of Christ. We
must be a light in the darkness. We cannot do
that if we're not living in unity.

Jesus, I want to be a godly woman. When I'm working with others, it's so hard for me to avoid arguments, even in a church setting. Help me to have a loving attitude.

God, often I don't realize I'm part of the problem when I'm just listening to gossip. I get interested in what's being said and it draws me in slowly. Before I know it, I'm commenting and making assumptions. Sometimes I even pass on the information whether or not I know it's accurate. Please, Father, help me to call this what it is. Gossip. It has no place within my church family. Please help me to realize that I'm getting involved sooner and give me the strength to stay out of it.

Heavenly Father, help me to build others up
rather than tear them down.

Lord, it's hard for me to give in when I have
a strong opinion of how something should be
done. It may be in the children's ministry or
even something as simple as how dishes should
be set out at a church dinner. Remind me
that these are trivial matters and that far more
important is my ability to get along with the
other ladies in my church fellowship.

God, if we argue within our church family, how
are we any different than the world? The world
sends us messages every single day that revolve
around self. *Do it if it feels right. Have it your way. Just
do it.* Your ways are not the ways of the world;
therefore, our church should stand out as a holy
place that revolves around love.

People are looking for peace. They can't find it in the world. You have told us that true peace can come only from You, Sovereign God. Just as the early church increased in numbers during a season of peace, I pray that my church will seek to humbly work together in love and consideration that we might be pleasing to You. Help us to be a peaceful church so that the lost might enter our doors and find Jesus here.

I want to sow seeds of kindness, joy, and spiritual truths. I want to be part of something bigger than myself. I want to use my gifts to further the kingdom, Jesus. Help me never to sow seeds of discord in my church.

How can we serve You, Jesus, when we are not serving one another? Give the women of my church servants' hearts. Set before us a picture of You washing Your disciples' feet. May we serve one another. May we serve tirelessly as Marthas in your church and yet never be too distracted to sit at Your feet like Mary.

Death of a Child

"Blessed are those who mourn,
for they will be comforted."
MATTHEW 5:4 NIV

There's an old hymn that says, "I need Thee every hour, most precious Lord." When a child dies, you need God like you've never needed Him before. You feel overwhelmed at first by shock, and then grief sets in and will not relent.

People don't know what to say, and they say all the wrong things. But you can't imagine what the right thing would be. There are no words. There is just deep, deep loss.

You brought this child into the world and you never dreamed you would bury him. You were his mother. You met his every need as an infant, and you taught him and guided him every day of his life. How could this be God's will? This feels like a horrible mistake.

In your days of deepest sorrow, God is there. He is with you every hour, every minute. He has not left you and will not leave you even for one second. Rest in His everlasting love.

Father, thank You that the waves of grief are just that—waves. Thank You for mercifully seeing to it that there are moments of relief. They're few and far between right now, but they do come. There are moments when I do not cry. There are moments when I'm able to smile or think about something else, if even just long enough to accomplish an everyday task. I thank You for those moments of relief.

No one hurts like I hurt. I was this child's mother. I felt the pains of labor when this life began, and I cry out in horror as I have been forced to watch it end. Thank You that despite this deep pain, I do know that in You there is no end to life. I will see my beloved one again in heaven. This is a promise I cling to today.

I know they mean well, but their words sting. Others just don't know how to deal with this. I don't either. Please help me to be gracious and forgiving when their words are all wrong. They mean well, Father. They know not what they do when they say these things to me.

Nothing makes sense anymore, Father. Thank You that it is enough for me to be silent before You. I have no words, and I cannot pray. Not today. Thank You for assuring me that it's okay to just be still and to be held close today.

I must eventually find a new normal. God, will You help me? This doesn't feel normal at all— trying to go on, trying to live when my child is not with me. I need Your help to make it through the day. I need You to help me find a new way to live.

Sometimes, God, it brings me just a bit of comfort to know that You lost Your Son, too. You watched Him hang upon a cross and die a terrible death He did not deserve. You gave Him up willingly for us. I can trust You because Your comfort is not just sympathy but empathy. You, too, have buried a child.

God, I know this grief is the price I pay for having loved with all my heart. I don't regret loving my child with the love only a mother can give. I would do it all again even if I knew it was going to end. I would love just the same. I would pour out myself just the same way. How I miss the privilege of being a mom to my child. Hold me, Father, as I mourn this deep, deep loss.

Death of a Parent

*"I will not leave you as orphans;
I will come to you."*
JOHN 14:18 NIV

Do you find yourself feeling lost or abandoned due to the death of your parents? Even though no family is perfect, parents are often the pillars or stability of a family unit. When they're gone, there's just something vital missing. There is a void. They were your *mom and dad*. Long before you carried many of the other titles you bear now, you were their *daughter*.

Even if your parents were old when they died, or even if your relationships with them were strained, it's life-altering to lose parents.

Know that God was not surprised by this. He ordained every day your parents would live on earth. He knew when it was time to take them home. He is there to help you as you move through this time of grief and into a future that will be different but will still hold joyful times and new blessings. He will never leave you as an orphan.

Father, I'm thankful for the memories, but they bring me little comfort today. Instead, they hurt. I miss my parent. I miss all the happy times. I pray that one day I'll be able to enjoy the memories again without the pain. Bring me through grief to the other side, I pray.

God, regardless of my parent's imperfection, this was the parent You gave me. In all our ups and downs, this was my parent still. Help me to honor the memory of my parent as I walk through this time of loss.

Father, I'm shaken by this loss. It's one that goes all the way to my core, for my parents were with me from the beginning. I don't remember life without them. Being their daughter came long before being a wife or a career woman. I really don't want to find out what it's like to be without them, but I have no choice. Help me, Father. I feel so sad today.

Dear God, I am who I am largely because of my parent, and now I am without this vital person in my life. Help me to remember all the lessons I learned just through doing life together with my parent for many years. Help me to forget the bad and to hold on to the good. Help me to honor my parent's memory by being a beautiful legacy as their daughter in this world.

Jesus, there are words I wish I'd spoken and hugs I wish I'd given. There are visits I wish I'd made more effort to make happen. There are cards that were not mailed and phone calls I was too busy to place. Please take away my guilt and remind me today of all the things I did do right for my parent.

I guess I always knew my parents may die before I did. It's sort of expected. But knowing it would happen and experiencing it are very different things. I had no idea how painful this would be. Give me the strength to walk through this grief. Give me love and support, I pray, at just the right moments, whether from my husband or friends or coworkers. You know exactly what I need in order to survive this.

Nothing comes to me that You have not allowed, God. Even this deep loss of my parent was ordained by You. Your Word says You have ordained each day that we live. You number them. My parent lived the exact number of days that You established. That brings me comfort. It reminds me that You are in control and even now, when nothing seems right, You are holding things together and will continue to do so.

Death of a Pet

Weeping may last through the night,
but joy comes with the morning.
PSALM 30:5 NLT

*P*ets are a special part of our lives. They're often even more faithful than humans in our lives. When a pet dies, there's a sense of grief just like when we lose a person in our lives. We grieve the loss, and this is normal. Even though some will say our pet was "just an animal," God understands the sorrow. He created a marvelous variety of creatures to fill His world with uniqueness and beauty.

When the time is right you can get a new pet, but there's no hurry or pressure. Take time to grieve during this difficult time. You'll walk through the stages of grief just as with any other loss, and one day before too long you'll be able to smile and enjoy happy memories of times spent with your pet. Let God comfort you with His love as you experience this sadness that is simply a part of having loved an animal friend deeply.

Dear God, I miss my pet. There's such an emptiness in the house. When I come home, I feel so alone. Please comfort me as I grieve.

When my husband was too busy with work, my pet was there. When the kids ran off with friends, I always had the company of this special pet. I was always enough for him. There was a special bond that I miss terribly now. I know You understand my sadness, God. Please help me move through this time of grief to the other side where I can smile again and perhaps even enjoy owning a new pet.

God, thank You for giving me my pet and allowing me to learn from this special little one. It seems silly to say that I learned from a pet, but I did. Thank You for the lessons I learned through being loved so completely by an animal. Thank You for the memories. I would do it all over again even though I have to experience this sadness and grief.

You created my pet, God. You breathe life into every living creature, and You know just how long we are to spend on this earth. I know You loved this little animal even more than I did. Thank You for that, Father.

Thank You, God, that I've been given a sensitivity to others who have lost pets. I've been in their shoes. I understand the devastating loss. Help me to be there for others when they are experiencing the pain of losing a beloved animal friend.

As the woman of the house, I was often the one who took care of our special pet's needs. I filled the food and water bowls. I made the vet appointments. I tried to teach the kids responsibility through pet ownership, but ultimately this pet depended on me a lot! I feel a little emptiness now that she's gone. I need to be needed the way she needed me. That may sound odd because I'm so busy as a wife and mom, but I miss caring for our pet. Bring me comfort and fill in that gap with Your love today, I pray.

God, may my children learn through this. May they realize that love often leads to loss but that it's always worth it. Teach all of us, Lord, to be open to loving another pet, I pray.

Death of a Spouse

Be merciful to me, LORD, for I am in distress; my eyes grow weak with sorrow, my soul and body with grief.
PSALM 31:9 NIV

When you made a vow for better or for worse, you never imagined this. You look back now and think how much you took him for granted. He was just there. And now he's gone. How could he have abandoned you like this? And yet, you know deep down you shouldn't blame your spouse. It was his time to go home to heaven. You just weren't ready to let him go.

Everything has changed. You're responsible for so many things that he took care of before. There's a dark black line that separates your life into two segments now—before he died and after he died. The words seem so foreign still.

Trust in God. He will be your rock. He will carry you when you can't go one more step. You will journey through the darkness of grief, but one day there will come a bit of light and then a bit more. You are going to make it. God is with you.

God, I never expected to be walking through this. It feels as if You've left me all alone. How could this be? It doesn't seem real. But I wake up day after day only to find that it is, in fact, very real. My husband is gone. I feel abandoned. Be my husband, I pray. I am so heartbroken. Be the lover of my soul. Fill in all the empty spaces with Your love, Jesus. I need Your help to make it. I cannot do this alone.

God, they made meals, but I could not eat. They sat with me, but I had no words to speak. I don't know how the hours passed because I'm just so numb. But I thank You that they came, these loving servants who have poured milk for my children and run errands and made necessary arrangements. Thank You that they came. They were Your hands and feet today.

God, nothing seems right anymore. No one says the right thing. I don't expect them to. There is nothing right to say. Everything feels off, and I feel so very alone. I need him. I didn't always appreciate him or tell him I loved him, but I need him, Father. He has abandoned me in this world. Bring me comfort, I pray. The pain is so deep, so intense. You are my only hope.

I was not a perfect wife, Lord. I wish I'd made more effort in some areas and held less tightly to a few grudges. Help me to know that no one is perfect. Help me to find peace in the sweet memories and to recognize that I did my best to be a good wife and he knew that. We didn't always say the things we should have. We thought we had more time.

Lord, thank You for reminding me through friends and loved ones to take care of myself. Others need me. You need me. I cannot lose myself completely in this. I must rely on You to see me through just as You've seen me through other seasons of difficulty. This seems too big, but nothing is too big for my God.

Thank You for the honor of being his wife. Thank You for a wedding day photo that captured the moment. Thank You for our children who have his expressions and his passion. May we live out his legacy in this world. Thank You for the time we had with this special man. Help us to trust Your timing even though it seems he left us far too soon.

Depression

He lifted me out of the slimy pit, out of the mud and mire;
he set my feet on a rock and gave me a firm place to stand.
PSALM 40:2 NIV

*H*ave you ever been in a dark house that was not familiar? Perhaps you were visiting a friend or relative and had to get up in the night to go to the bathroom. You find yourself stumbling, bumping into furniture and walls. You don't know the way through the darkness.

When you get there and flip on the light, everything becomes clearer. You remember that the dresser is situated just next to the door and you can see again that the countertop juts out a bit farther in that one spot.

Depression is like this. When you come through to the other side—and you will, with help and with time—things will seem clearer. Right now, when your life feels shrouded in darkness, simply trust in the dark what you have seen in the Light. Hold on to Jesus.

I've been here before, God. Depressed. I know that last time there came a brighter day. You lifted me out of the pit. You took away the veil and revealed joy again. . .slowly at first, and then one day I could hardly remember the depressed state I had walked in for so long. Bless me with recovery again. Heal my mind and heart, I pray.

I cannot imagine singing. I can barely get my shower and see to the duties of the day. But I have faith in You, Lord. One day I'll be on the other side of depression and I'll sing a new song. I'll tell of how You healed me and lifted me up. I'll sing a new song and it will be one of great joy and deliverance (Psalm 40:1–3).

Heavenly Father, why is my soul so cast down?
Why do I feel such turmoil? Help me to hope in
You. I know I will again praise You, for You are
my salvation and my God (Psalm 42:11).

This is not my home. This world is full of
trouble, including depression. But You,
Jesus, have overcome the world. One day I will
experience an existence in heaven that does
not include the pain of darkness or this sick
feeling of hopelessness. That will be a place of
great hope. For now, there are troubles. You
will walk us through them. I will keep my eyes
on You, and one day I will be fully and forever
free of these bouts of depression. That will be a
glorious day! (John 16:33).

God, give me wisdom. I don't always know what's best, and everyone has a different opinion on such things as counseling and medication. I know that I need help and admitting it is the first step. Help me to have the presence of mind, even in my depression, to make the best decisions that will help me to get well.

I feel like a failure, God. A loser. A bad Christian. I feel like an awful employee because of my lack of focus. I feel like a pitiful wife and mother because I'm so sad all the time. I feel beat down. Please remind me of my identity in Jesus Christ. I claim today that I am deeply loved and that I am not a failure. Bring healing to my mind today, Jesus, just as You healed the bodies of those who dared to reach out and touch Your robe.

Disabilities

And a woman who had been suffering from a hemorrhage
for twelve years, came up behind Him and touched the fringe
of His cloak; for she was saying to herself, "If I only touch His
garment, I will get well." But Jesus turning and seeing her said,
"Daughter, take courage; your faith has made you well."
At once the woman was made well.
MATTHEW 9:20–22 NASB

She reached out and touched the hem of Jesus'
robe. She was a woman who had been living with
an illness for many years. She knew what it was
like to be left out, to suffer, and to long for life
to be different. Jesus healed her in an instant
because of her great faith.

God chooses to heal some from diseases
and disabilities in this life, and others He will
heal when they enter heaven one day. We know
that one day we will have new, flawless spiritual
bodies. There will be no more pain or crying in
heaven. The blind will see. The lame will walk.
The deaf will hear.

Disabilities draw men and women closer to
God. Those with handicaps must rely on Him
in ways others rely on themselves. Complete
dependence on God is a very good thing for
anyone to learn and live out in this life.

God, sometimes I think I fear that which I don't understand. I see people with certain disabilities and I'm not sure how to react. Please help me to be loving and kind, treating everyone with respect and as I want to be treated. You love all of us, regardless of our race, age, or if we have a disability or not. Each of us is made in Your image.

Lord, I feel like I'm on a roller coaster with this disability. Some days my emotions are stable, and I feel good. Other days I feel far from "normal," and I just wish I could do all the daily tasks that others do so easily. Please steady my thoughts and feelings. Help me to trust You to meet my needs, even with this disability, day by day.

You are the great physician, Father. Whether You choose to heal me in this life or wait until I'm in heaven with a brand-new body, I trust You. I know that You will use this area of my life to grow me closer to You. My faith is stronger because I must look to You every day. Draw me close, and remind me that You are my confidence.

Dear heavenly Father, sometimes I feel like all I can do is deal with this disability. I feel like daily life is somewhat of an obstacle course for me. I watch others who don't have disabilities, and I find myself feeling envious. Please remind me that everyone I meet is fighting some sort of battle. We are all imperfect and weak creatures in need of a strong God to carry us. Thank You for being my Savior and friend.

I know that people see me as different and some of them feel sorry for me. I sense it when they stare. Some look at me in a sad way as if they don't know what to say. I want to thank You for my differences, God, even though at times they are a real challenge. They make me more sensitive to those around me. I realize all of us have special needs. Some are on the outside and some hide within. Help me to look at others with a smile and kind eyes.

Father, I want to help those with disabilities. Show me what I can do even if it seems like a small gesture. Guide me to an opportunity within my church or community. Perhaps I could keep children with special needs while their parents attend Bible study. Maybe I could help out with Special Olympics. Direct my path, I pray.

Disappointment

Though the fig tree does not bud and there are no grapes on the
vines, though the olive crop fails and the fields produce no food,
though there are no sheep in the pen and no cattle in the stalls,
yet I will rejoice in the LORD. I will be joyful in God my Savior.
HABAKKUK 3:17–18 NIV

*Y*our disappointment may be in others or in
circumstances beyond your control. It may even
be in yourself. You may have hoped to be married
by now, and yet there is not even a prospect.
Maybe you had career aspirations that have had to
fall by the wayside due to responsibilities as a wife
or a single mother. You imagined life one way but
you're living it out in quite another.

Disappointment is a part of life. It's how you
respond to it that makes the difference. Will
you cave when things don't go your way? Will you
wallow in self-pity or despair? Or will you yet
praise your heavenly Father who promises to
work all things together for good in your life?
Praise Him even when nothing seems to go
right. Closed doors lead to open windows. God
is not finished with you yet.

Father, I'm not where I thought I would be in life. I imagined things differently. I knew a prince would not ride in on his white horse, but I never expected my reality to be quite this mundane. There are dishes to be done and a house to keep clean. The laundry piles up around me. I pray that I'll work at everything I do today as if I'm working for You. Give me a contentedness in the midst of disappointment.

Lord, You know that things haven't turned out as I wanted. You saw the dream as it grew within my heart. You watched me get my hopes up. You were there as I held my breath, hoping for the answer I wanted so desperately. I wonder why You let it all slip through my fingers. Remind me that Your ways are higher than my own (Isaiah 55:8–9) and that You always have my best interest in mind.

Jesus, this test feels more like a dead end than just a bump in the road. I'm so disappointed. Yet I know that this trial will strengthen my faith and instill perseverance in me, helping me toward completeness (James 1:2–4). Please use even the disappointments in my life to make me more like You.

Like Mary and Martha who waited for You to come and heal Lazarus, my jaw drops when You don't show up to rescue me or provide what I desire. Remind me that You are never early or late but always right on time. What feels like a disappointment is only a detour that will take me to something greater.

Father, when You close a door in my life, You always open another one. Right now I'm so fixated on this one piece of the puzzle, but You see the completed picture. You know what is best. Help me to seek Your will.

Some trust in chariots—or, in present-day life, social media "likes" or promotions at work! I choose to trust in the Lord my God. When I feel let down and discouraged, remind me that You are my strength and my fortress. I am more than a conqueror through Christ.

God, I like the song that says "You are more than enough for me." I want that to be true in my life. When my husband lets me down, when my children frustrate me, when my job is a disaster, You are more than enough. Please teach me to hold loosely to the things of this world that I might put my hope in You alone.

Discontentment

*I know what it is to be in need, and I know what it
is to have plenty. I have learned the secret of being
content in any and every situation, whether well
fed or hungry, whether living in plenty or in want.*
PHILIPPIANS 4:12 NIV

*E*ven the apostle Paul had to *learn* the secret
to being content. It was not natural or innate;
rather, it was *learned*. As we face circumstances
that are less than desirable and find God there
in the midst of our disappointment, we are
strengthened in our faith. Can you look back
to another time in your life, whether long ago
or fairly recent, when God came through for
you? He is in the business of making a way where
there seems to be nothing but a dead end. That's
how our God works.

So during this season of lacking or despair,
look up. In this hopeless hole, claim hope in
Christ your Redeemer. It may seem that you've
been given the short straw or that life is nothing
but a cruel joke. You may be nowhere near
where you want to be today. But trust the heart
of God. He is working out His plan in your life.

God, when I see someone who is old or sick or in some way disabled, I often find in their eyes a sense of contentment. I see it in the way they smile or offer a word of encouragement to someone else—even though they themselves are not doing all that great. Help me to find that kind of contentment. I don't think my countenance reflects peace. I want it too, Father.

You were the King of the universe, and yet You were content to be laid in a manger as a baby. You were content to live an adult life in which You never really had a place to call home. You were content with the role God gave You. You asked Him to take the cup from You in the garden that night, and yet You were content to carry Your cross to Calvary for me if it was God's will. . .and it was.

God, I know that contentment begins with an attitude change. I haven't been able to make it. I see glimpses of it at times, but my overall outlook is bleak, not sunny. I need to find a place of contentment. Show me the way. It seems so overwhelming, so out of reach. Show me just a small step that I can take today to become more content.

Circumstances dictate my level of contentment. It shouldn't be that way but honestly, it is. When good things happen, I'm a happy Christian, praising You in church and singing and praying throughout the week. When hard times come, I blame You. I ask where You are. I turn away. Funny how when I come back around, You are always there. You haven't moved. I'm the fickle one. Create in me a more content spirit that I might be faithful to You regardless of my situation or my station in life.

Help me, God, to just hold on and "fake it till I make it." As I express gratitude to You for all of Your blessings, help my discontentment melt into appreciation for Your provision. If I have to force myself to thank You for three things each day, I will, Father. In time, I believe You can change my heart.

Thank You, God, that You promise in Your Word that You will never withhold a good and perfect gift from those who walk with You (Psalm 84:11). My emotions are getting the best of me lately. I begin to believe, at times, that You don't want me to be happy. You seem to be keeping me from my dreams! I know that I can trust Your heart, though, and that this is just a lie Satan wants me to believe. Help me to trust that You are in control and that although You have closed these doors, You surely will open the right ones that You are preparing for me.

Distrust

I will trust and not be afraid.
ISAIAH 12:2 NIV

Trust is a tricky thing. It's learned. And once one learns to withhold trust, that distrust is hard to "unlearn." We learn to trust our parents or caretakers. If they don't prove trustworthy, our sense of stability is shaken. It may be a spouse that you trusted who let you down, or a dear friend who became someone you didn't know she could be.

God wants you to learn to trust in a healthy manner, with boundaries. He knows the pain you've experienced and the fear you have of ever trusting anyone again. That's no way to live, though. That's like living in a prison even though you're not physically behind bars.

Trust God today. He is always faithful. He will heal the parts of you that have trouble trusting.

God, I trusted once, but I was let down and betrayed. I don't know that I can open my heart to anyone else. I have tried, but I keep putting up the walls again and again. Please help me to trust You so that I can learn to trust others.

I say that I trust You, God, but deep down I hold on to the reins. I won't quite surrender all the control over my life. I try to control what happens in my work and my family. I don't delegate well because I don't trust others to come through for me. I just try to do it all myself, but it's not working for me! Help me learn to trust so that I can depend on others and upon You, Lord. It's a lonely and difficult life without trust.

I know that there's an abundant life waiting for me. I get glimpses of it at times. I start to make commitments and decisions but then, like a mouse, I run back into my hole! How can I know for sure that things will turn out well? How can I trust that these people won't change their minds or give up on me? I'm tired of living like this. Please help me to learn to trust.

God, I feel like I should apologize to You because I don't trust You. You are the Maker of the universe, and You created me. I believe that. I know that even though I only see in part, I am fully known by You. And yet, how is it that I can't seem to trust that You know the plans You have for me? Help me to relax and believe that You have a bright future in store, plans to bring me hope not harm (Jeremiah 29:11).

Father, I want to trust You with all of my heart. I want to learn to lean not on what I understand, but in all of my ways to acknowledge You and to submit to Your will. I know that when I trust You, You will make my paths straight before me. You will lead me and never let me go (Proverbs 3:5–6).

There are those who can and should be trusted in my circles, Father. There are also some who cannot and should not be trusted. Grant me discernment in this area that I might know the difference. I need to know when to trust and when to guard my heart, but it's not always easy to see the wolves in sheep's clothing. Show me those people in whom I should trust, I pray (Psalm 5:9), and help me to stay far away from those who wish to hurt me.

Divorce/Separation

For I am convinced that neither death nor life,
neither angels nor demons, neither the present nor
the future, nor any powers, neither height nor depth,
nor anything else in all creation, will be able to separate
us from the love of God that is in Christ Jesus our Lord.
ROMANS 8:38–39 NIV

*I*f you're facing divorce, regardless of the circumstances, you are hurting. You may feel that this is a failure or sin that God cannot redeem in your life, but that's not true. We are promised in the book of Romans that God will never leave us. Nothing, not even divorce, is able to come between you and the love of God. You are fully loved even though you feel incomplete at this point in your life.

Divorce is never God's first choice. It's not His plan or His desire that marriages should end before one of the spouses is called home to heaven. But for many reasons, some beyond our control, divorces do happen. You stand in the midst of broken dreams for a bright future with your husband, but God stands ready to help you in the healing process.

God, it all just happened. It seemed to spiral out of control, and then there were papers making it legal. . .and he was gone. The end had come, and I hardly even had time to say good-bye. Sometimes I wish he had died. I know that's an awful desire, but I guess death is just "cleaner," more clear cut. This type of grief is so confusing because my husband—my *ex*-husband—is still living. Help me, Father. I am so confused and sad.

God, I need You. I can't make it through the day without You. Things that used to seem easy and mundane are taking all of my brain power in order to accomplish. Everything in my world has been shaken, and it seems so odd that the sun still comes up and everyone is moving on as if nothing happened. Help me make it through each day, Father. I feel so useless and out of control.

God, help me not to be bitter about this divorce. I know that bitterness can grow up and fester in my heart and that it has the potential to ruin my life. I have seen others allow this to happen, and I don't want to be like them—sitting around talking about this for years to come. Give me strength to grieve well and then to move forward well. Thank You, Father.

I know You still love me, God, but I don't know why. I feel so used up and worthless now. I feel like all the promises and dreams are just gone, over, done with. What happened? I glanced at a wedding photo today. Where did those happy smiles go? I had so hoped things would turn out differently.

I feel like I need some help, Lord. I don't think I can move past this without assistance. If there's a certain friend or counselor I should turn to, please put that person in my path. Make it clear to me, I pray, if I should attend a support group. I want to heal, Father, and I need help.

Help me to make wise choices when I consider whom to confide in about my divorce. I need to talk it through, and yet I don't want to discuss it with all of my friends. I can't reveal details to everyone. It isn't even right. My marriage was a private thing until this happened. Now I feel like everyone is wondering what happened and looking for answers. Help me to know when to speak and when to remain silent, Father. Give me discernment as I choose a friend whom I can trust to listen and remain confidential.

Doubt

If you don't know what you're doing, pray to the Father. He loves to help. You'll get his help, and won't be condescended to when you ask for it. Ask boldly, believingly, without a second thought. People who "worry their prayers" are like wind-whipped waves. Don't think you're going to get anything from the Master that way, adrift at sea, keeping all your options open.
JAMES 1:8 MSG

Do you go before God in confidence that He is *with* you and that He is *for* you? Do you believe that He exists and hears your prayers? We are commanded to go boldly before our heavenly Father's throne, fully acknowledging His power to do great things. The Bible warns against doubting. While certainly we all doubt from time to time, God can help you to be sure of Him if you just ask.

We are told that with faith the size of a mustard seed, we have the power in Christ Jesus to move mountains!

God, forgive me for doubting You. I don't
want to be like Thomas who demanded tangible
proof. He wanted to see the nail scars in Your
hands before he would believe You. I find myself
feeling like that at times—wishing You could
come down here and chat with me for a while,
assuring me You have my future under control.
Your Word gives me all the promises I need. I
know that. I want to believe. Help my unbelief
(Mark 9:23–24).

God, help me to build my house upon the Rock
of Christ Jesus, not on shifting sands. I know
that there is no stability in doubting. I want
my hope to be steadfast and true. You are the
Alpha and the Omega, the beginning and the
end. Help me to trust You with these and with
everything in between.

Father, I want to have faith like the men and women I read about in the Bible. Often, I trust only in what I can see before me. I realize that You call me to faith in that which I have not yet seen (Hebrews 11:1). It's really not faith if I only believe in the tangible. I must trust in the intangible. All around me there is proof that You exist. Help me to count my blessings and to construct altars along the way so that I can remember times You came through for me (Genesis 35:3).

When I begin to doubt You, Lord, bring to mind all the times that You have answered my prayers. Sometimes this helps me to remain calm and trust You even in the midst of circumstances that seem impossible. You are the God of the impossible. You are strong and mighty, sovereign and faithful. I trust You, God.

Heavenly Father, I've been doubting again. I lie in my bed at night and wonder if You even see me here and know my needs. I doubt Your love for me because of how things have turned out. This is not the life I had planned for myself. Give me the ability to see beyond today to the future that You have in store for me. Help me to believe that You are not finished with me yet.

Father, thank You for Your promises in scripture that I can claim throughout my trials. You promise to never leave me or forsake me. You assure me that nothing—absolutely nothing has the ability to separate me from Your love (Romans 8:38–39).

Drug Abuse

*Do you not know that your bodies are temples of the Holy
Spirit, who is in you, whom you have received from God?
You are not your own; you were bought at a price.
Therefore honor God with your bodies.*
1 CORINTHIANS 6:19–20 NIV

*T*aking drugs does not honor God. He
put your body together in a mysterious and
miraculous way. He breathed life into you,
and all drugs do is suck the life out. If you have
accepted Jesus, you have the Holy Spirit dwelling
within you. He is your Counselor. You sense
that what you're doing and the dependence
you've developed are wrong. Make the choice
today to seek help for this disease of addiction.

God wants you to be well. He wants you to
shine for Him. You can't do that when you're
weighed down with substance addiction. Right
now all of your focus goes toward when you'll get
your next high. Can you imagine the freedom
that you could experience if you walked away
from that life? God has extended His mighty
hands to you. Leave drugs behind. Seek a new
life starting today.

Lord, keep me sober. One day at a time. One hour at a time. I know that my body is not my own. I was created by You and for You. Help me to honor You with my body. Give me the strength I need to turn away from drugs.

God, You are not trying to keep me from having a good time. Help me to realize that the "good times" I've been chasing aren't good for me at all. Renew my heart and help me to want the things that are good for me. Drugs are repulsive. Why do I keep going back to them? Help me, God, before it's too late.

Jesus, in You I am free. Help me to use that freedom in productive ways. I want to make a difference in the world. Drugs cause me to be selfish. I want to learn to be selfless. Heal me from this dependence. I want to be used for Your kingdom.

God, You have called me to be salt and light to Your world. When I'm abusing drugs, I can't be either of these. I want my conversations to be seasoned with fervor for You. I want to shine as a light for You in the dark places of this world. I could even help others to get off drugs. Please continue to keep me sober so that I can be salt and light, I pray.

Lord, I know Your voice. Help me to tune into the voice of my Master, my Good Shepherd (John 10:27), not the other voices that call to me. The world is full of pleasures that wind up as disasters. There's a new promise for a greater high or escape every day in the places I've been living. Help me to escape this dangerous obstacle course and exchange it for the straight paths You've prepared for me.

God, I don't want sin to reign over me. You are my King, not drugs. Bring me back from the dead. Make me alive again in my faith and in my walk with You as Savior and Lord of my life. I want to be Your instrument of righteousness (Romans 6:12–14).

Create in me a clean heart, God, and renew in me a steadfast spirit (Psalm 51:10).

Dysfunctional Relationships

To all who mourn in Israel, he will give a crown of
beauty for ashes, a joyous blessing instead of mourning,
festive praise instead of despair. In their righteousness, they will
be like great oaks that the L ORD has planted for his own glory.
ISAIAH 61:3 NLT

*R*elationships are complicated at best.
Whenever two people enter into a relationship
of any kind—parent to child, husband to wife,
brother to sister, friend to friend—things get
messy. We are all fallen beings, sinful and
imperfect. When you add layers of issues such as
divorce, loss, disappointment, and crutches or
addictions, things can get extra complicated. . .
often dysfunctional.

Know that the Father sees the heartache
of your relationships. He knows that you want
things to be better even if you don't know how
to go about making the necessary changes. He
knows the regret you feel each time that old cycle
comes around again. He wants to bring beauty
from ashes. Seek Him. He is the one true God,
the one who is capable of the impossible.

God, some of this is not my fault. Help me to see the parts I do need to take responsibility for and make the necessary changes. I want this relationship to be better, and yet I keep doing and saying the same things. Wanting is not enough. I must take action. Guide me, I pray, and help me to see my part in it all so that I can change it.

Give me a new heart, God. I need one. I'm so angry and hurt, and I try to control this relationship but I always fail. You are the only way, truth, and life. Please renew my efforts today and give me a brand-new heart toward the people involved (Psalm 51:10).

Heavenly Father, I hear about boundaries, but I don't even know what they would look like in my world. I'm constantly doing everything for everyone, trying to please, trying to keep the peace. I know this isn't healthy. Teach me where I need to establish healthy boundaries, Father. Give me the opportunity to take care of myself so that I can have something left over to give to others.

God, I heard it said once that you won't get a different result if you keep doing the same things over and over again. I feel like I'm caught in a bad dream. My loved one and I keep having the same issues, the same fights, the same dysfunction between us. Please give me discernment so that I might see a new way. I'm tired of these same old results.

Jesus, I need help. I need a counselor or someone really wise to guide me. I don't know who I can trust and who can give me sound, biblical advice. Please show me where to turn so that I don't have to bear this alone any longer. This relationship is destroying my life.

God, I can't admit this to my parents or siblings. There is not a single friend I feel that I can turn to with the depth of this dysfunction in my marriage. I'm embarrassed. I didn't know it could get this bad. I had no idea when we took our vows how hard it would be for me to keep them. Please help me. Show me someone I can trust who can help us through this. Things have to improve, and I believe they can. . .with Your help.

Elderly Parents

Listen with respect to the father who raised you,
and when your mother grows old, don't neglect her.
PROVERBS 23:22 MSG

I always knew this time would come. The roles are reversed. I'm taking care of my parents in the ways they once cared for me. It seems so strange. My parents were always so capable. They never needed me for anything. Now they do.

Please give me patience to listen to that story just one more time. Please give me the words to say when I know we must make a change, such as taking the car keys or moving out of their own home. Please help me to love my parents well and to honor them as You have commanded in Your Word. Please help me to take time to enjoy my parents as they grow old. One day they won't be with me any longer. I want to look back with no regrets.

God, You knit my parents together in their mothers' wombs. You have been with them all of their lives. I know You will remain faithful through this life and the next to keep Your promises to them. Thank You for their long lives and the blessing that my mom and dad are to me.

Father, it's not always easy to know what to do. I want my parents to enjoy independence as long as they possibly can. But I'm scared when things happen that could prove unsafe for them. As I make tough decisions for my elderly parents, please guide me and give me wisdom.

Jesus, You were a servant leader who even washed Your disciples' feet. Please give me a servant's heart, too. If I need to help my parents with things like bathing or going to the restroom, allow me to know how to assist while helping them feel okay about it. I want them to have their dignity. I love them so.

Gray hair is a crown of glory, which is gained by living a godly life (Proverbs 16:31). Help me to remember to honor my parents to their very last days. They have earned and deserve my respect.

Father, I pray that You will give my parents bright spots today. Even as their bodies are beginning to fail them, I know that You remain faithful and true. Give them neighbors who care and joyful moments such as watching birds out their kitchen window, just little things to cheer them through the day. Thank You, Lord, for loving my mom and dad.

Even in the Old Testament, You made sure the people knew that they were to respect the elderly. Your law told them to stand in the presence of their elders (Leviticus 19:32). I'm so thankful for my parents, and I want to show them the respect they are due.

Enemies

*"You're familiar with the old written law, 'Love your friend,'
and its unwritten companion, 'Hate your enemy.' I'm challenging
that. I'm telling you to love your enemies. Let them bring out the
best in you, not the worst. When someone gives you a hard time,
respond with the energies of prayer, for then you are working
out of your true selves, your God-created selves. This is what
God does. He gives his best—the sun to warm and the rain to
nourish—to everyone, regardless. . . . In a word, what I'm saying
is, Grow up. You're kingdom subjects. Now live like it. Live
out your God-created identity. Live generously and graciously
toward others, the way God lives toward you."*
MATTHEW 5:43–48 MSG

To whom much is given, much is required.
How many times have you failed? How much sin
did Jesus take to the cross for you? The grace is
immeasurable, the generosity unbelievable.

The Message puts it in modern terms here
in the book of Matthew—"grow up." Don't
argue with those who differ from you in politics
or even religion. God loves Democrats and
Republicans alike. He loves those who have
accepted Him and those who are still lost. It is
our responsibility as Christ followers to follow
His lead in this. Jesus prayed for those who
persecuted Him. Go and do likewise.

Jesus, help me to fight evil with good. Give me the strength to take a deep breath and show love even to those who are not easy to love. I read about how You asked the Father to forgive those who crucified You. That's unbelievable to me, and yet, I'm called to love and pray for my enemies as well. Help me, I pray.

Heavenly Father, I pray right now in this moment for the ones who have hurt me. I lift them up by name before Your throne. Perhaps they truly "know not what they do." I know that hurt people are known to hurt people. Please heal the wounds in their souls. Please use me as a representative of Your grace and generosity.

God, I'm so quick to defend myself sometimes. The tongue-in-cheek comment or sarcastic remark that comes my way from a coworker is rarely ignored. Often, I retaliate. I am quick to speak. The comebacks fly! Take control over my quick tongue, Father. I pray that I will stop and think before I speak. Sometimes saying nothing is far more powerful.

Holy Spirit, be my Comforter. I've been wounded by someone who really knows the buttons to push. I'm filled with hate and, in my own strength, I'm unable to muster up love for this individual. I need You to be strong in my weakness. Replace my anger with compassion.

Help me, Jesus, to consider this person's perspective and the hurt within that must drive these careless wounds he inflicts on others. I pray for healing in his heart.

You emphasized a lot of things in Your teachings, Jesus, but the greatest was love. Love is a powerful force capable of changing a heart. Your love changed my heart. Use me, I pray, to be a living example of unconditional love to others today—especially those who are my enemies.

You are the God of the impossible, Lord. You are the maker of every heart. You have the power to soften hearts and turn enemies into fast friends. Be a miracle worker in this situation, I pray.

I want to be more like You, Jesus. Amazingly, You treated Your enemies with respect. You loved them. May I not be overcome by evil, but instead, by the power of Your Spirit, may I overcome evil with good (Romans 12:21).

Facing Death

For to me, to live is Christ and to die is gain.
PHILIPPIANS 1:21 NASB

It's hard to imagine that death is actually better than life. For the Christian, this is true. Every man and woman will one day face God. When your final breath is taken on this earth, you will enter into eternal celebration or damnation. The Bible makes that very clear.

If you have Jesus in your heart, death is not something to fear. The moment you leave this body, you will have a brand-new one in heaven. The moment you draw your final breath, the party will have just begun welcoming you to your eternal reward. To live is Christ. To die is to gain eternity in His presence. Surrender your fear of death today to the One who made you and has ordained each day that you will live upon this earth.

God, it's easy to say one doesn't fear death—until it's knocking at the door. I know I am drawing closer and closer to the time when I will take my final breath. Please reassure me that while death is "the final enemy," You have already defeated it! I will live forever with You in heaven.

Heavenly Father, I entrust my family and friends into Your care. For so long, I've worked and tried to care for them. I've given all that I can. My time draws near. Please take care of them for me as I have to leave them behind.

The valley of the shadow of death never seemed so real as it does today. I will not fear it. You are here with me, just as You promised to be. You protect me. You comfort me. I will live forever in the house of my Lord (Psalm 23).

I am fully known. You put me together in my mother's womb. But I have walked through this life with only a glimpse of who You are. My humanity has kept me from knowing fully. There are secret things that simply cannot be understood in this life. I'm coming close to the time when I will know! I will know fully just as I am fully known. I look forward to that, Lord (1 Corinthians 13:12)!

You died, Jesus. You died upon the cross. You died, just as I am dying here in this place now. You took a final breath, just as I will soon. But hallelujah, You did not stay in the grave! Because of Your death, my sin was forgiven and I was made right with God. Thank You for dying for me that I might have eternal life.

I am in the garden, Jesus. I'm praying for another way. I'm asking my Father that the cup might pass, that I might not have to drink the bitterness of death. But my body fails me, and I grow weaker. I know deep down that He is going to take me home soon. Give me the acceptance that You had when You realized Your death was not an option but a certainty. I want to go in peace to my eternal home.

Failure

See how great a love the Father has bestowed on us,
that we would be called children of God; and such we are.
1 JOHN 3:1 NASB

Abraham and Moses failed. Peter and Paul made serious mistakes. David failed, and so did Elijah. But God used their failures to carry out His will for them and to bring them to where He wanted them to be.

You are a precious daughter of the Lord Most High. You are cherished by Him. Does your love for your own child decrease when he or she comes up short? Does a failure on your son or daughter's part cause you to be any less his or her mother? Certainly not!

God loves you not because of how many times you get it right or wrong but because you are His child. You are saved by grace through faith in Jesus Christ, and you appear as righteous before your heavenly Father. Failures and successes will both come your way. Learn to accept this. God always accepts you—regardless of how many times you may fail.

I want to be successful. Who doesn't? I want to do well in my career and climb the ladder. I want to be a good friend and coworker. And yet, I fail. I let people down. I miss deadlines. I come up short. Remind me that You love me not one bit less when I fail than when I am victorious. Thank You for Your unconditional love, God.

My failure leads me to repentance. I come to You when I fail. I seek You. When You say You work all things together for good for those who love You, I think that includes our failures. If I were always a winner, I would not rely on You as much. I fall into Your arms when I fail. You are always there, steadfast and true.

Sometimes I refuse to try because I'm afraid I'll fail. I did this as a child and I thought I would outgrow it, but I haven't. Instead of avoiding a sport or activity, I now avoid bigger things—like relationships and job applications. Give me confidence, Father, and strengthen my spirit so that it's okay even if I do fail.

My identity is in Christ Jesus. I am saved and loved and cherished. My identity does not depend on how well I do things. Remind me of this, Father. Thank You for loving me so unconditionally.

God, Peter denied three times in one night that he even knew You. I would call that a failure. And yet, You still used him. You understood His humanity. Use me, too, I pray, in spite of my weakness and failures.

Use my failures to help me improve, Lord Jesus. When I yell at my children, use this to teach me patience next time. When I miss a deadline at work, teach me to prioritize better in the future. I can improve. Help me to have the confidence I need to do better next time.

The world may call me a failure, but You see it quite differently, Lord. I'm in this world, but I'm not of it. I'm an alien here, for my real home is heaven. When I don't have the largest bank account because I've given freely to others, remind me that money is not the most important thing. When I choose to stay in a place where I'm making an impact for the kingdom, remind me that this honors You. It's okay to let an opportunity for promotion or change pass by if I'm where I feel I should be. In Jesus' name I pray for confidence to do what's right regardless of how the world may view it.

Family Feuds

Above all, love each other deeply,
because love covers over a multitude of sins.
1 PETER 4:8 NIV

*T*here are family squabbles, and then there
are family feuds. Certainly every family has its
disagreements and arguments. When you put a
bunch of different personalities together, these
will occur. The real trouble comes when the
disagreements grow into deep-rooted fights that
keep us from loving one another well.

Examine your role in the family feud. Are
you the instigator? Do you stir up trouble?
Or do you stand by and say nothing when you
could make a difference if you spoke up to the
ones continuing the argument? Do you even
remember where this all began?

Pray for God to make a change in the course
of your family's path. At this point things are
not going well, but God can bring about great
change. Ask Him for guidance and watch as He
intervenes to save your family even from itself.

You offer a peace that the world simply cannot. It's a peace that comes only through a personal walk with Your Son, God. It's a peace that my family needs desperately. Please bless us with a peace that passes all understanding. I ask this in the powerful name of Jesus.

Please help us turn our barriers into bridges. Please help us to consider the others' perspectives. God, I ask You to please heal our wounds. Bind them up. Change us from the inside out. We need You, Lord.

God, You use broken vessels. You use broken families. The families of the Bible were far from perfect. Find my broken family useful to Your kingdom, God. Cause us to consider how much better our passion would be spent on spreading the Gospel rather than feuding among ourselves. We've been angry for so long that I'm not sure any of us even remember how it all began. Forgive us, God. Change us. Use us, I pray.

Jesus, my own family has hurt me so deeply. I don't feel like forgiving, but I know it's Your command. I know that I should forgive seventy times seven times. I know that I cannot be healed unless this war within my family comes to a halt. Please guide me in how to help that happen. It needs to happen soon, Lord.

God, help me to place You above my family. Family is important, but I know that You are more important still. When I cease to find my worth in what my relatives think of me, perhaps I'll be freed up to love them and forgive them for the ways they've hurt me. Help me to find my identity in You.

Family Stress

As pressure and stress bear down on me,
I find joy in your commands.
PSALM 119:143 NLT

*S*tress is a quiet enemy. It's not evident like a roaring lion but rather sneaky like a serpent. It slithers into a family and chokes out the life and laughter that was once abundant. It often comes not in a big, bad force but in the form of too many good things. For example, there is nothing inherently wrong with a child playing on a soccer team, another competing in gymnastics, a working mom, or a dad whose job requires occasional travel. But put all those together and you might have a recipe for disaster.

Whatever activities and habits have combined to create such a high level of stress in your family, you simply must take careful inventory and do some house cleaning. Just as you clean out the clutter of old clothing and toys, rid your family of some of the pressures so that joy can breathe again among you.

I can't remember the last time we sat down together for a meal. We are coming and going. The work and school schedules are only the beginning. All the extras are what seem to steal our time. Remind us of what's important, God. Help us to prioritize better. We need some down time, some time to enjoy being a family again. I pray that You'll guide us as we determine what we should cut out in order to lessen our family's stress.

The stress I'm experiencing is beginning to take over my family life. We used to laugh and play games together. Where did we go wrong? God, I know that I often lash out at my husband or the kids when they don't deserve it. I let my stress overflow and become my family's stress. Forgive me, Lord, and help me to manage stress better so that it doesn't ruin my family.

Help us to slow down, God. The hurry and the busyness of everyday life can be so consuming. Please grant my husband and me discernment as we make choices for our family. Maybe one sport is enough for each child to play. Maybe one of us should turn down the overtime even though it puts a dent in the bills. Family is more important than extracurricular activities or money. Give us wisdom, Father, to know what to say yes to and what things we'd be wise to say no to.

God, I see my children's stress. I hear it in their bedtime prayers. I miss their easy smiles and silly laughter. We're going through a tough time. Help us to shield our children as much as possible so that adult stress doesn't impact our little ones like this. It breaks my heart, and I know that You don't want them to be so burdened.

God, I pray that You will guide us as we analyze what's causing the stress we're facing. We know this is not how You want us to live. We must determine what to do about it. Grant us the ability to make changes where changes are possible. Help us to learn to live peacefully and to find creative ways to work around the stresses we cannot eliminate.

Jesus, help us not to play the blame game but to seek a solution for this stress we're facing. We have to work together on this.

Family is such a gift. Help us to remember that throughout the year, not just on special occasions like birthdays and Christmas. Help us to be kinder to one another, God. I don't want to look back in years to come and see a family torn apart by daily stresses. I want our family to be strong. Help me to do what I should do as the woman of this home to help make us a strong family again.

Fear

"Do not fear, for I am with you; Do not anxiously look about you, for I am your God. I will strengthen you, surely I will help you, Surely I will uphold you with My righteous right hand."
ISAIAH 41:10 NASB

*H*ave you ever seen a man being protected by a bodyguard? The bodyguard tends to be a great deal larger and stronger. The man, whether he's a celebrity or the president of the United States, can go about his business. He doesn't have to look this way or that. He need not fear that which he doesn't see as he shakes hands and makes speeches. Why doesn't he fear? Because his bodyguard is watching. His job is to protect. His job is to lay down his very life if necessary.

This type of protection is amplified by millions when you consider that the God of the universe watches over you. He tells you not to fear. He is with you. You need not look to the left or right. He will hold you up with His righteous right hand. Bank on that promise. Do not fear.

Lord, as a woman, sometimes I feel afraid and vulnerable. I fear being alone. I fear failure. I fear opening up, loving and trusting others. I fear things I have no business fearing. You tell me in Your Word that each day has enough trouble of its own and that I need not borrow trouble. Set a guard over my heart, Father, so that I will not fear things I shouldn't. Calm my spirit, I pray, that I might rest in You again.

God, You are my refuge and strength, an everpresent help in trouble (Psalm 46:1–2). Because of this, I choose not to fear, regardless of what happens. Even the worst situations will not cause me to crumble. You are in control. You will work all things together for my good.

Jesus, I've been afraid. I'm tired of fearing silly things—things that are out of my control. You graciously offer me peace—Your peace. It's a peace the world knows nothing of and cannot offer me. If I simply receive Your peace, I know that my heart will not be troubled or afraid (John 14:27).

Abba Father, when I lay my head on my pillow at night, I will rest in the knowledge that my Creator is in control. I have nothing to fear. You watch over me as I sleep. You have promised never to leave me. You sing over me as I sleep. The powerful, peaceful lullaby of my God.

You are with me, Lord, so I will not fear. I have You, and because of this, I need not fear what others may do to me. My God is on my side (Psalm 118:6).

You have given me a spirit of power, of love, and of self-discipline (2 Timothy 1:7). I am not alone. You go with me into battle. The battle is not my own. It belongs to my God. I refuse to fear. I call on the powerful name of God Almighty to see me through. Thank You for fighting for me, Lord.

Financial Strain

*My God shall supply every need of yours
according to his riches in glory in Christ Jesus.*
PHILIPPIANS 4:19 ASV

*A*s you look out your window in the morning
and see the birds fluttering about, do you see
fear and worry in their eyes? Do the flowers
tremble, worrying how they will survive? How
silly! Of course not! God sends the rain. He
provides food for the birds. He nourishes
the flowers through the soil in which they are
planted. How much more will He care for you!
You are His precious daughter, bought with the
blood of Jesus.

When money is tight, ask God to stretch
it. Keep living and giving. Budget and remain
conscious of your spending, but remember that
ultimately God is in control and He will provide
for your needs. You can trust in Him.

Jesus, money is tight. I seem to run out of it before I run out of days in the month. Please take what I have and stretch it. Give me wisdom in my spending and in places I can cut back. Ultimately, help me to trust You with this money. It's all Yours anyway.

God, just as You take care of the lilies of the field and the birds of the air, You will take care of me. You know my needs. I don't have to scurry about or worry excessively about money. I simply need to lay this burden down and trust You. You have come through for me before and You will do so this time. I thank You for taking care of me so well (Matthew 6:28–33).

Dear Jesus, help me to continue to give even when there is not as much in my bank account. I know that giving is a blessing to others, but it's also a blessing to the giver. I know that You will provide for me as I continue to follow Your command on my life to give (Luke 6:38).

God, I have not been wise with my money. You know that I have wasted money on things that did not honor You. Help me to make better choices as I move forward. I want to do better and to honor You with my spending. You are the giver of all good gifts. Give me the self-control to use my money in ways that will further Your kingdom and not be wasted on things of the world.

Help me to be content with much or with little. My bank account does not define who I am or the degree of happiness in my life. Whether I find myself wealthy or poor, help me to honor You and to be thankful to You for what I have (Philippians 4:11–13, 19).

God, I give You my finances. I should have done so a long time ago. I thought I had the money under control, but I didn't. It began to get away from me little by little, and here I am in debt that's swallowing up not only me but my family with me. Forgive me and help me, God. I give it all to You, and I ask that You help me to sort it out and to do better with financial responsibility in the future. I want our family to honor You in every area—our finances included.

Going through Change

*C*hange is a natural part of life. Very little stays the same. Whether you're experiencing a change associated with joy or sorrow, you will need to rely on God to help you adjust.

As women, we crave routine and sameness. It makes us feel secure. A sense of stability is very important to us. When something changes in our lives, it may leave us feeling unsettled or afraid. Remember that Jesus experienced change. He left heaven to come down to earth and be born as a baby—not in a royal palace but in a stable for animals. Talk about change! He understands the jolt that a sudden shift in one's reality can bring.

Pray that the Holy Spirit will enable you to embrace rather than resist change. Change can be a glorious thing, opening new avenues and bringing new adventures that you might have otherwise missed.

God, I don't like change. I'll admit it. I like the comforting feeling of knowing what each day will bring. This has brought some anxiety into my life. Please help me to look to You to help me adjust.

Father, this change has caught me unaware. I wasn't ready for it or expecting it. I didn't have time to prepare. Please come alongside me and show me the way I should react to it. Give me grace to accept it and to find the positives even though it's an unwanted change in my life.

God, I know that not all change is bad. It can be invigorating! Today I pray for a new perspective. Help me to embrace the changes that have come my way. Help me to enjoy them even.

Some people seem to thrive on change. They move frequently and take new jobs. They enjoy variety. I wish I were more like that. I like routines and regularity. This change has shaken up my nice, predictable world. I find myself in a panic. Calm my spirit, Father. Remind me that You have not left me. We will walk through this time of adjustment together. Thank You for being near.

God, I know there is one thing that will never change. You will never leave me. Even if my job changes. . .even if I must move across the country. . .even if I'm abandoned by others. . . even if I grow ill or disabled and cannot live the way I'm used to. . .You will be there. You will never leave me or forsake me (Deuteronomy 31:8). I take great comfort in Your faithfulness and loyalty, heavenly Father.

There is a time for everything and a purpose for everything that happens (Ecclesiastes 3:1). I know this change is not a surprise to You, Lord. You see all the pieces of the puzzle that make up my life. I can only see one piece at a time. You see how this "new normal" is going to draw me closer to You and how it will challenge and shape me. Please allow this change in my life to bring You glory, just as everything should. I love You, Lord.

You know the plans You have for me, Sovereign God. Your plans are never to hurt me but always to bring me hope. You have a good future in store for me (Jeremiah 29:11). Help me to look at this change as just a part of the plan. Thank You for assuring me that You are still in control even when things seem a bit out of control in my little world.

Grief

l are those who mourn for they will be comforted."
MATTHEW 5:4 NIV

*G*rief follows when we lose someone to death, but we also grieve for the living. We can even grieve dreams that didn't turn out as we had imagined. Perhaps you were abandoned by a parent or by your husband. In many ways, the one who left you is dead to you now. You must walk through grief. If you've experienced abuse, you must grieve your innocence or the trust that once came so easily. You may have had your childhood stolen from you at a young age due to sexual abuse. Grief is the result.

Recognizing that grief comes as a result of loss is very important. Whether you've lost a dear relative or friend to death or experienced another type of loss, grief is natural. You'll be in shock or denial. You'll feel anger and sadness. You may try to bargain with God. You'll pass through the stages of grief. But one day you will recover. The loss will still be there, but the pain will lessen. Trust God to walk with you. Ask Him to hold you close as you grieve. Cry out to Him. He is there.

Dearest Lord, I'm grieving a loss that was long ago. It comes back to me at certain seasons of the year. A situation or a phrase can catch me so unaware. I find myself transported back to another time and another place. The loss feels just as deep and the grief just as strong as it was back then. Comfort me with Your Holy Spirit, I pray. This is a deep loss, and I must not try to brush it off as less. I must acknowledge the pain so that You can provide a healing balm to my soul.

I need You, God. I can't walk through this alone. I'm grieving for one who still lives. It's harder, I think, than grieving for the dead. This person is not part of my life anymore, but this is not my choice. I simply must accept the decision another has made and walk through the grief that is the result. I can't control all of the losses in my life. Walk with me, God. We can do this together. I can do it if You stay with me and assure me that You will never leave.

Jesus, I'm filled with grief. I feel like I cannot go on. I've lost a part of me. I don't feel like me anymore. Hold me close. I know that grief is the price we pay for love. I pay it gladly. I would love again just as fully even knowing that this is how it would feel in the end.

I have loved and I have lost. It's part of the human existence. The beauty of grieving for a believer in Christ is that we don't have to grieve as the world does. We grieve as those who have hope! We will see our loved one again. We will be together in heaven for all eternity. This is just a "see ya" rather than a final good-bye.

Grief is like a roller coaster, Father, and I'm so tired of riding. I want to forget. I want to get off this tumultuous, up-and-down cycle. And yet, I know that shutting down my emotions is not healthy. I must ride this out. Will You come with me? Will You sit beside me so I can cling to You when I'm afraid? I need You, Father, as I ride out this deep period of grief.

I'm grieving the loss of a friendship, Lord. I remember when this friendship was light and fun, a positive thing in my life. But that was a long, long time ago. You have clearly shown me it was time to walk away. I know that ending this relationship was best for me. But it doesn't take away the sadness I feel. It's hard to let go of someone I love.

Guilt

Blessed is the one whose transgressions
are forgiven, whose sins are covered.
PSALM 32:1 NIV

The Lord forgives. He is your hiding place. He will not let the waters reach you and overtake you. He keeps His loving eyes on you and guides you and instructs you. He protects you from trouble and surrounds you with songs of deliverance.

These are all promises found in Psalm 32. To claim this freedom and victory in Jesus, your part is simply to confess. Sounds easy enough. . . but sometimes we carry unnecessary guilt for far too long when we've done something wrong.

Learn to go to God quickly. Be honest with Him. He has seen your sin. He knows you through and through. There is no hiding iniquity from God. Sometimes confession of guilt is a very difficult and emotional thing for a woman. We must not avoid it, though. Just as we plunged into the waywardness that led us here, we must plunge into the forgiving arms of our Lord. What comfort there is to be found in the arms of Jesus!

Jesus, You paid a debt I could not pay. I was guilty of sin. You were a spotless Lamb, without blemish. You took upon your shoulders the sin of the whole world. You died a terrible death as the innocent Son of God to make a way for guilty sinners like me to come into the presence of a holy God. I am forever grateful to You for paying my debt.

Remind me today, God, that I can't change the past. I feel guilty for the things I've done and the people I've hurt. Transform these feelings of guilt into encouragement to move forward as a changed woman. Wallowing in my guilt will not do any good, but praying for the strength to do better in the future will.

I confess my sin to You in these moments, loving Lord. I fall before You, weary from the burden I've been carrying. I release it all to You. I am so sorry for my sin. It hurts my heart to know that my sin hurt You and displeased You. Lift this load of guilt, my Savior. Forgive me, I pray.

Lord, sometimes when I feel guilty, it comes out in other forms. I grow angry. I'm short with those I love. I avoid people or places that remind me of my sin. All of these things impact others around me. They're not healthy for my marriage, and they don't strengthen my bond with my children or grandchildren. My coworkers suffer as well. Father, please forgive me and help me to walk as a forgiven daughter of the King as I move forward.

Thank You, Lord, for not counting my sin against me. Thank You for washing me white as snow through the blood of Jesus. I don't have to hang my head in shame or guilt. Jesus died once and for all. A supernatural stain lifter, He removed my guilt. Hallelujah! I am free.

I know, Father, that I cannot keep Your laws perfectly. If I break even one law, I've broken them all (James 2:10). That's why I need a Savior. That's why I need Jesus. Forgive me, I pray, and wake me up tomorrow ready to face a new day in a new way.

Thank You, God, that when You look at me, You see me through a Jesus lens. Perfect and blameless, clothed in righteousness, forgiven and free.

Hidden Sin

*When I kept silent, my bones wasted away through my groaning
all day long. For day and night, your hand was heavy on me;
my strength was sapped as in the heat of summer.*
PSALM 32:3–4 NIV

*H*idden sin is not really hidden at all. You may attempt to keep it from others or even from God. It never works. When the heart of a believer is not at peace with God, it shows in her countenance and in her interactions with others.

Secret sin festers and enlarges in our lives. It causes us to lie, and one lie always leads to another. Even lies of omission are dangerous territory. Not telling the whole truth is just as bad as directly lying.

Jesus wants you to find freedom from your hidden sins. Bringing them into the light is the only way to experience true forgiveness and peace. Whatever you are struggling with, He stands ready to forgive and help you move forward as a new woman. Do it today. Go to Jesus. Confess. Go to those you've been hurting as a result of this sin. Make things right. A burden will be lifted. You will feel as if you've been given new life!

God, this hidden sin eats away at my heart. I have no peace because of it. Help me to give it to You. Help me to run from it so that it will not have any power over me any longer. The temptation is great, but I don't want to return to it anymore.

Father, there are no secrets with You. You knit me together in my mother's womb. There I was still just a secret, and You knew me even then! What makes me think I can hide sin from You? I choose today to bring this hidden sin into the light. Forgive me, Lord, for hiding from You as Adam and Eve did in the garden. I want to be right with You again.

There are habits that I've developed that don't line up with who I say I am. I go to church on Sunday and worship You through song, but my worship stops at the door. I'm leading a double life, and I want to come clean before You, Father, and before my family. I am so tired. Please give me the courage to confess.

Examine my heart. If You find any wicked way there, bring it into the light. I don't want anything to come between You and me, Father.

Nothing is covered up or hidden. In the end, all will be known (Luke 12:2).

Keeping up the act is a drain on me. I act one way but I'm covering up what lies beneath the surface. My thought life is not what it should be, and lately some of my actions have frightened me. I feel like I'm just one step away from blatant rebellion. Draw me back to You, Father, before it's too late. This secret is destroying my life.

I come before You with dirty hands and a dirty heart. I know that the wages of sin is death. I feel as if I'm a dead woman somehow still walking around among the living. I confess this sin to You, Father. *[Speak the sin or sins you have been hiding from God here.]* I ask You to forgive me in the powerful name of Jesus and set me on a new course for my life.

Infertility

Hannah was in deep anguish, crying bitterly as she prayed to the LORD. And she made this vow: "O LORD of Heaven's Armies, if you will look upon my sorrow and answer my prayer and give me a son, then I will give him back to you."
1 SAMUEL 1:10–11 NLT

There are many longings in this world, but there is perhaps no greater longing than some women have for a child. Not all women want children, but most have maternal instincts that cause them to desire motherhood. When this goal is delayed or denied due to infertility, it can be nearly unbearable.

If you are experiencing the pain of not being able to get pregnant, you are not alone. Many, many women have been in your shoes. You may be surprised by a miracle baby that comes to you either biologically or through adoption. Try to trust God during this season. Know that He is always for you and never against you. A longing for a child is very natural. Trust God through this trial that He sees your longing. He has not forgotten you.

Lord, help me to give this longing to You. Help me to surrender it. I have laid down other dreams over the years. This one is perhaps my deepest desire. I really want a child. Help me to trust You more as I wait and as I live with this longing.

God, I know You are a God who works miracles. You are able to do the impossible. I ask You to allow me to become pregnant if it is Your will that I bear a child.

Be with my husband. He wants a child, too, but we are so different as we react to infertility. Please help this draw us closer together rather than drive us apart.

I remember playing dolls as a little girl, God. I never dreamed I wouldn't have a house full of children when I grew up. Now I would give anything just for one child! Please fulfill this desire of my heart if it's Your will for me.

I'm not sure who to be angry with—You, my husband, myself? I'm just angry. I can't stop feeling so frustrated. It seems so easy for other women to become pregnant. Not me. Why must I be the odd one out? Why is it impossible for me to have a baby? Calm my heart, God. I'm so upset, and I know that this is not Your desire for me. You want me to trust You more.

God, they are everywhere—pregnant women and women with newborn babies. Please help me to rejoice with others and to celebrate new life. I don't want to be a jealous person. My heart longs for motherhood, but even in this difficult place I pray that I can be happy for others.

I know that You *can* allow me to get pregnant, but I guess I wonder if You *will*. So far, each month I get my hopes up, and each month my hopes are dashed. You are the giver of life, and I know that if and when You desire for me to have a baby, You will bring about a pregnancy. Help me to believe that You will do whatever is right and best for our family.

Heavenly Father, I surrender this longing. I lay down the desire. I'm weary from this burden. I'm tired. I can bear this alone no longer. I need You to help me. I need You to calm my spirit and dry my tears. I am sad and frustrated, but even still, I will praise You, my Creator and Sustainer.

Insomnia

When you lie down, you will not be afraid;
when you lie down, your sleep will be sweet.
PROVERBS 3:24 NIV

*I*nsomnia can be a real problem. As a woman, you feel so responsible for so many others around you—your husband and/or kids, those you work with, friends going through hard times, aging parents. . . The list goes on. When you can't sleep, all of your worries are amplified in the sleepless dark hours. And when you get up in the morning, you are unable to be at your best for those who depend on you. It is such a vicious cycle!

You may dread going to bed because you fear you will yet again face the frustration of lying there awake again. Anxiety overwhelms you, and you feel out of control.

But God's love never fails. He has compassion on your sleeplessness. He wants to help rid your mind of fear and worry. Pray that He will give you sweet sleep. God wants you to rest in Him.

Sovereign God, my mind is racing. Please slow my thoughts and bring a calm over me. As I lay here in bed, please let my breathing fall in rhythm with Your spirit. Let me sense Your nearness. Bring to my mind all the times You've protected me and blessed me in the past. I know that I have nothing to fear because You watch over me.

Lord, take away the worries that multiply in my mind when I lie awake. As each anxious thought overtakes me, let me turn it over to You. You tell me to cast my cares upon You because You care for me.

Dear God, I want to lie down and sleep in peace. I want to believe that You will keep me safe (Psalm 4:8). Above all, I want to just close my eyes and fall asleep. It's a goal that seems unattainable to me even though it comes very naturally for others. Please grant me a good night's rest tonight, I pray.

God, I cry out to You. Sustain me. Lay me down to sleep. Awake me again tomorrow, refreshed (Psalm 3:4–5).

As a child, I would pray, "Now I lay me down to sleep." Lately, sleep does not come easily. I find myself tossing and turning. By the time I fall asleep, it's almost time to get up again. Father, I need You to help me. Give me peaceful sleep, I pray. Just as I slept as a child, without a care in the world.

Father, I need Your peace to guard my heart and mind (Philippians 4:7). I need You to help control my emotions. They spin out of control when I'm tired. Help me to sleep. Restful sleep makes such a difference in my ability to face daily trials. I'm a better wife and mother when I get my sleep. Please allow me to find peace and to sleep well tonight when my head hits the pillow.

God, insomnia is common. Help me to remember that this is not unusual and that normally, with time, it will pass. Many people struggle with it. I am not alone. In the hours when I can't sleep, please remind me to use the time to pray. I've been blessed in some of those quiet prayer times spent with You while my husband and children are asleep.

Jealousy

The acts of the flesh are obvious: sexual immorality, impurity and debauchery; idolatry and witchcraft; hatred, discord, jealousy, fits of rage, selfish ambition, dissensions, factions and envy; drunkenness, orgies, and the like. I warn you, as I did before, that those who live like this will not inherit the kingdom of God.
GALATIANS 5:19–21 NIV

One of the first words a little girl speaks is "mine." We are quick to announce what belongs to us and perhaps even quicker to want what is not! Like one toddler grabbing another's toy is the woman who gazes upon what her friend has in envy.

Are you struggling with jealousy? It's subtle at first, but left unattended it can overtake your entire life.

When you feel that little green monster creeping into your thoughts, say a prayer. Tell God that you're thankful for your friend, and ask Him to give you a heart that celebrates her victories and is happy for her accomplishments.

Lord, You know the desires of my heart. Help me to be happy for others when they are successful or receive blessings or rewards. Just because all of the longings in my own life are not yet fulfilled, I don't want to be bitter about others' victories. Help me, Father, as I struggle with jealousy.

As I look at other women, God, I admit that I'm sometimes envious. I look at others' lives and find myself wanting what they have when I should appreciate my own blessings. Keep me focused on the positives in my life, the things others may long for that I have been given. These may be things I take for granted that others would love to have. Replace my envy with a heart of gratitude, I pray.

God, I remember the story of Joseph and his colorful coat. Joseph's brothers were jealous of him and sold him into slavery. You were with Him through it all and You rescued him. You showed him favor and gave him great wisdom. You raised him up as a leader in Egypt in spite of his brothers' intentions. Work in my life, too, Father. I'm being mistreated because of someone's jealousy. It's out of my control, but nothing is out of Your control. I ask You to work on my behalf (Acts 7:9–10).

Father, I know that You are a jealous God. You desire that I have no other gods above You. Where am I spending most of my time and money? These may be areas of my life that need close examination. Please help me to eliminate anything that threatens to become a god in my life.

I remember the old song that offers this advice: "Count your blessings. Name them one by one. Count your many blessings. See what God has done!" There is no time like the present for me to stop and do just this. Thank You, Father, for each of these blessings in my life. Thank You for ____ [list the blessings in your life]. I am so very blessed.

God, I see my girlfriends' families on social media. They all look so perfect and happy. Meanwhile, my own is struggling. I see their profile pictures. They seem so pretty and put-together. I never look like that! I've gained weight, and I'm looking older these days. It's so easy for me to compare myself to others. Please help me to realize that while my life is not perfect, neither are theirs! Help me not to grow jealous of my friends but to pray for them and to recognize the blessings in my life.

Job Stress

*Work willingly at whatever you do, as though you
were working for the Lord rather than for people.*
COLOSSIANS 3:23 NLT

*Y*ears ago, women did not have jobs outside
the home. Times have changed, though, and
many women today are juggling the responsibilities of work in and outside of the home.
Stress on the job can lead to stress at home,
and vice versa. It's important to remember to
whisper prayers throughout the day and remain
close with God even as we work. This will keep
our hearts in the right place and often will stop
conflicts or stress dead in their tracks.

Each day as you begin your work, commit it
to the Lord. Ask Him to bless your work and to
calm your heart and spirit, trusting in Him to
help you even with mundane tasks and meeting
deadlines. Work with dedication and integrity as
if God were your boss. After all, He is!

God, thank You for my career. Thank You for giving me a job that I enjoy and one that suits my gifts. Help me to find a balance, though, between work and home. I don't want my family to suffer because I'm stressed out about work.

May the words of my mouth be pleasing to You. I struggle with this. When I'm tired and stressed, I often fail to speak to my employer or my employees in a way that honors You, God. Help me to take a deep breath in those times and whisper a prayer. Help me to remember that my tongue has the power to lift others up or tear them down. I want to honor You with how I speak in my workplace.

Lord, there just aren't enough hours in the day. Help me to know how to prioritize. Give me the wisdom to know if I should cut back my hours or even let this job go at some point. I truly want to put my family first, but we need the income this job provides. Lead me, Father. I want to honor You in my work.

God, as a woman, I feel so torn. I want to be the best at everything, but so often, due to overload and stress, I feel I'm letting everyone down. My husband, my children, my boss, and my coworkers. Show me how to balance my time. Remind me that often the work can wait and needs to be laid down at a certain time so that my family life does not take second place.

At times I feel like everyone and everything is against me. I can't please my employer no matter how many hours I put in or how hard I work. Remind me, Lord, that You are for me. If You are for me, who can be against me? (Romans 8:31).

I come before You, Lord, and I admit I'm not in a very good state. I'm stressed out and overworked and tired, so tired. It's in moments such as these that I refocus. I find You there. You never moved. It was I who drifted. I look up and find my Father's face smiling down at me. You offer me an easy yoke. I accept, Abba Father. I will rest in You.

Loneliness

My soul, wait in silence for God only, for my hope is from Him.
PSALM 62:5 NASB

*I*f you're single, you may be lonely for a husband. If you have a husband, you may be lonely in your marriage. If you have children, you may be lonely when they're away or you may think of the days when you were unencumbered by motherly duties. You may miss running around with your girlfriends, footloose and fancy free. You may be lonely for those friends who don't come around much anymore now that you're changing diapers or driving carpool. If you live alone, you may be lonely for companionship. If you live with others, you may be lonely even in their presence. Loneliness does not always mean alone. You may be painfully lonesome even in a crowd of people.

If you rely on man to fill the God-shaped hole in your heart, you will find that the puzzle piece never quite fits. You'll remain lonely, and you'll grow tired of working aimlessly at filling the void.

Learn to seek God. Be still before your Maker, your Redeemer, your Best Friend.

He is the only one who can fill the lonely crevices of your soul.

When I call to You, You answer. When I am in trouble, You come running. You are with me. That is such a comfort to me, God (Psalm 91:15).

God, I'm lonely. There are so many things I want to do, but often, I can't think of anyone who would want to go and do them with me. I long for a close friend. Please help me to find a new Christian friend. Remind me, oh Father, that even if I have hundreds of friends, I need You more than any other.

Heavenly Father, he lies next to me in bed but I'm lonely. He sits at the same dinner table with me, but I can't think of things to say that will engage him. We've grown distant, and I'm so lonely in my marriage. Please help us, Father. Please help me to reach out. Show me how to connect with my husband again, I pray.

You will not leave me. You have called me by name. You call me Your own. When I pass through deep waters, You will not let me drown (Isaiah 43:1–5). Loneliness overwhelms me, but You are still here with me. You never look away. You never wander. You are my God, always near. For that I am so very thankful.

Help me, Lord, to reach out to those who may be lonely today. It often helps me to do something for others. There is always someone worse off than me, someone I can minister to, someone who could use a friend. Show me the opportunities You have for me to be a light today.

This is a lonely season for me, Father. I remember a time when my life was full of people. Things have changed. I find myself alone more often. Use this season, Lord, to draw me closer to You. Let me fellowship with my Father when I'm alone. As a Christian, I'm never really alone, for You are always near. You will be with me always, even to the end of the age (Matthew 28:20).

God, I'm busy all day with my children. My home and vehicle are filled with my own kids and their friends and classmates almost all the time. How can I still feel lonely? I think I miss adult conversations. I need friends in my life again. Thank You in advance, God, for helping me to find some time for me—outside of being Mommy.

Moving

"Remember that I commanded you to be strong
and brave. Don't be afraid, because the LORD
your God will be with you everywhere you go."
JOSHUA 1:9 NCV

*M*oving can be exciting, but often it brings at
least some degree of difficulty and stress. You're
leaving behind what you know and stepping into
the unknown. Will you have friends in the new
place? Will your neighbors be nice?

Even though the old house had its issues,
you're used to its creaks and quirks. You'll miss
them! There will be new and unfamiliar sounds
in the new home. You're not sure you can
adjust, but you will.

As you leave one place and head toward
another, recognize that God goes with you. The
house is just walls. God abides within your heart.
He will dwell with you in any place that you may
call home for the rest of your life. Embrace
this move. Choose to step into change with
confidence that your God has gone before you
to prepare the way.

There is a time for everything. There is a season for everything that happens under heaven (Ecclesiastes 3:1). I loved our home, but this is the time to move. We made a lot of memories there. I'll miss some things about it, but I will not look back. I will look forward (Isaiah 43:18). You have moved us, and we are following You, God.

My heart is torn, God. Part of me wants to stay, but the other part knows it's time to move on from this place. It's hard to step into the unknown, but I know that You go with me. Please prepare the way for me. I will walk in it. I choose to trust You in this move, Father.

I remember when we moved into this house, God. It was new to us then. The rooms seemed empty and big. Gradually we filled up this place with children and stuff and more children and more stuff. It's so familiar now. I don't even need the light on to move from room to room in the night. This house has been a good home for us, and I'll miss it here. But You've called us to a new place. There will be empty rooms there, but we'll fill them up with "us." Soon it will feel like home. Soon I won't have this sick feeling in my stomach the way I do today as I say good-bye to our house.

God, I'm scared. I've resisted this move and dug in my heels, and even when the house sold easily and You provided the new one, I remained stubborn. There have been so many signs that this is Your will, but I'm just afraid. I need You to give me peace about this move, Father.

I won't know the neighbors, Lord. I won't know where the closest post office is or the best dry cleaner to use. I'll have to change doctors and grocery stores, and the kids will have to start at a new school. So many changes, God, and change is not easy for us. Please hold us close.

Help me to be positive about this move, Lord. Even though the circumstances are not ideal, help me to trust You. I need to be strong for others who are looking to me for their own strength in this move, God. Please give me a smile and a countenance that displays confidence that can come only from You.

Overwhelmed

The righteous cry out and the LORD hears them;
he delivers them from all their troubles.
PSALM 34:17 NIV

*I*t's no wonder that women often feel
overwhelmed in today's society. Many are
juggling a job outside the home along with
the duties of being a wife and mother. Others
are single moms who must balance a career
with raising children on their own. Some have
climbed the ladder in major corporations or
built their own businesses, working far too
many hours each day. Older women may be
overwhelmed by the responsibility of raising
grandchildren they never imagined they would
be called upon to raise.

Regardless of your circumstances, know that
you can turn to God. He understands. He's
ready to help you. Sometimes all we need is a
good cry! God gets that. He's there to listen and
to comfort you. Other times, we need to sort
through the stress in our lives and make some
necessary changes. Ask Him for guidance, and
He will gladly show you the way.

I'm overwhelmed today, God. You've seen my to-do list! Something needs to give, but I don't know where to make the changes. It seems that everything is equally important. I have to work so that my family can have income, but I have to be there for my kids or they'll feel I don't love them. Show me the way. I ask this in Jesus' name.

I come to You. I am burdened and weary. I need the rest that can only be found in You, Jesus (Matthew 11:28).

When I'm overwhelmed, You are the One who knows the way I should turn (Psalm 142:3). Show me, Father. I'm ready to make some changes to reduce the stress in my life.

I'm so overwhelmed by all of life's demands on me. Before I begin my work, I'll stop and spend time with You. I choose to put You first. I choose to rest in You so that You will bless the labor of my hands. I need You, God.

I remember a demonstration where a jar was filled with sand and then rocks were added. All of the rocks would not fit. But when the rocks were put in first, the sand was poured in and everything easily fit into the jar. God, help me to get my priorities straight. If I spend time with You first thing each morning, the rest of my day will flow much more smoothly, and You will multiply my time that I might do all that I need to do.

When You return, I want to be busy about Your kingdom work. I don't want to be snowed under beneath a pile of work and deadlines. I don't want to tell You, "Oh, Jesus, I wasn't ready for You yet. I have too much to do. I'm so busy. Can You return another day? I need a bit more time." Help me to live each day as if it were the day You were returning for me. I will live differently if I keep my sights set on that day!

God, my husband and kids don't seem to care. They hear me say how overwhelmed I am, and yet they continue to ask more and more of me. I need a break. I need help. Show me ways that I can delegate some of the chores. Show me how to confront my family and insist upon their help without being mean-spirited. I can't do all of this on my own. I really need them, God.

Prodigal Children

So he got up and went to his father. But while he was
still a long way off, his father saw him and was
filled with compassion for him; he ran to his son,
threw his arms around him and kissed him.
LUKE 15:20 NIV

*H*ow you wish your child would come to his
senses as the young man in Luke did. You may
find yourself experiencing a range of emotions
these days—anger, frustration, compassion,
sadness. When you pour yourself into a child
and he rebels, it's difficult to accept. You find
yourself doubting things will ever change. You
haven't seen your son or daughter in so long that
it seems this prodigal child will never return.

In the long hours of the night when you
cannot sleep, pray. At that moment when the
photograph of happier days catches your eye,
pray. Never give up praying for this child who
has gone astray.

You trained up a child in the way he should
go. He will not soon depart from it. He may
wander off the path a bit, but in time he is sure
to find his way again.

This child is Yours, God. You blessed me with her and I gave her back to You. I trusted You with her all these years. Why would I try to take her back now? You know my daughter better than I do, better than she even knows herself. Please protect her. Please lead her back to the right path.

I look back with rose-colored glasses, but I know there were some rough times as I was bringing up my children. I was far from the perfect mom. Please forgive me for the times I failed them, God. Please draw us back together. I miss them so.

Jesus, You told the story of the prodigal son. I imagine the father holding his tongue, fighting the urge to tell his son what a terrible mistake he was making. He let him go. Give me the grace to let my children go their own way. They're adults now and must make their own decisions.

God, I want to do something. I've always been a mover and a shaker. In this situation, I can't take control. I can't make things happen. I just have to pray. Help me never tire of praying for my children. There is great power in prayer. Remind me not to see it as a last resort. Keep me diligent in prayer and consistent in hope.

What Joseph's brothers meant for evil, You used for good. You can use my child's choices in his life. They seem wrong to me, but I must trust You with this child of mine. You work all things together for good in the lives of those who love You.

Heavenly Father, my children know Your voice. I taught them about You and took them to church. They know the Bible and its truths. Your sheep know the sound of Your voice. Guide these little ones back to Your ways, Good Shepherd. I ask that You call out to them. I pray that they will heed Your call.

Regret

Brothers and sisters, I do not consider myself yet to have taken hold of it. But one thing I do: Forgetting what is behind and straining toward what is ahead.
PHILIPPIANS 3:13 NIV

The apostle Paul who penned these words in a letter to the Philippians had a sordid past. He'd been a killer of Christians. Looking back would do nothing but bring him deep regret and sorrow. He had no time for such things. He was about kingdom work. He was preaching the Gospel and spreading the good news of Jesus.

If you have asked God to forgive you, He has done so. It's as simple as that. You're a clean slate. Now turn from the past, go toward your future, and let God write upon that slate as He will. Commit yourself today to focusing on Jesus and you will find that the troubling regrets you've been carrying will fade away. *"Turn your eyes upon Jesus. Look full in His wonderful face. And the things of earth will grow strangely dim in the light of His glory and grace."*

God, I keep looking back. I know You've forgiven me, but I'm struggling to forgive myself. This sin seems bigger than others. It seems like something I should pay for and keep paying for the rest of my life. Help me to accept that Jesus paid the debt for all my sin and that I'm forgiven and loved. I am a new creation in Him.

I've broken one of Your commandments, O Lord. I have not been a godly woman. No one knows the secret I bear. But You know. It burns within me, and I feel like maybe it would help to tell someone. Please guide me to a trusted person if this truly would help me. I'm filled with regret, and I wish I could go back in time and change things. I can't. Please hold me close, Father. I feel so undeserving of Your love today.

If I confess my sins, You are faithful to forgive
and cleanse me of all unrighteousness (1 John
1:9). I don't have to live with regret. It's a burden
You desire for me to lay down at Your feet. Help
me to do just that, God, and give me the strength
to move on rather than pick it up again.

Give me a glad heart, Lord Jesus. A glad heart
makes a cheerful face. I've been weighed down
far too long with sorrow. My spirit has been
crushed by this deep regret over what I've done.
I long to be happy once again (Proverbs 15:13).

I look to You, Sovereign God. I trade a countenance that reflects regret for one that shines with the radiance of my God. I am forgiven and free (Psalm 34:5).

I'm deeply sorry for the way things turned out. I wish I could turn back the hands of time and change my actions and hold my tongue. I wish I could make different choices. I wish. . .but wishing can go on and on, and still nothing changes. I heard it said once that if we spend too much time dwelling on the past, we will miss the present and have no future. I don't want that to be me, God! Help me to release the past and take hold of the future that You have in store for me. I want to be used in a mighty way for Your kingdom.

Self-Esteem

Therefore, there is now no condemnation
for those who are in Christ Jesus.
ROMANS 8:1 NIV

*Y*ou are precious to your heavenly Father. He was not fully satisfied after He created Adam. God chose to create woman as well. He gave Adam a helper. The Lord brought her out of Adam's rib and created her in His image. And He created you. He chose you as His beloved daughter. He saved your soul, watching His only Son, Jesus, die upon the cross to do so.

You could not be more loved. He loves you unconditionally on your best days, and on your worst exactly the same. He's not measuring your value according to your outward appearance, the amount of money in your account, or the type of clothing you wear. He's not counting the number of "likes" you receive on social media or the number of friends who click on your profile each day.

You are your God's pride and joy. You are His masterpiece. One day He will gather you to Himself in heaven. Jesus has gone there to prepare a special place for you. For today, surrender your troubles with self-esteem to him.

You are fully loved, and you need no other to love you. You belong to the God of the universe. He hugs His daughter close and says to call Him *Abba* which means "daddy." Find your worth in Him and in Him alone.

God, I want to trade my low self-esteem for Christ-esteem. Make me confident in who I am through Christ. I wrestle with dark spiritual powers of evil, but You are greater than these (Ephesians 6:12). Remind me of my salvation and of my great worth in Christ Jesus.

Father, I'm not sure what's causing me to feel so poorly about myself. Please examine my heart and reveal to me the ways my attitudes about myself need to change. I want to be a confident woman of God who is free to share Christ with those around me.

You knit me together in my mother's womb. I am fearfully and wonderfully made. Wonderful are Your works, Creator God (Psalm 139:13–14).

God, You don't look at the outward appearance but at the heart. You are not concerned with my height or weight. You don't see as men see. You see who I am on the inside. Remind me that my heart is what matters most. Thank You for loving me the way You do, Lord.

There is so much pressure in society for me to look and dress a certain way. I just can't keep up! God, You tell us in Your Word that our adorning should be the hidden person that I am in my heart—a gentle and quiet spirit, which is precious in Your sight (I Peter 3:3–4). Remind me that outward appearance is not all it's cracked up to be!

You know the number of hairs on my head
(Luke 12:7). You created me in Your image
(Genesis 1:27). Charm is deceptive and beauty
is vain, but a woman who fears the Lord is to be
praised (Proverbs 31:30).

I look around at my girlfriends and my husband
and even my own children. They all seem to
have such wonderful gifts and abilities. What is
mine? I know that I do a lot to help others, but I
sometimes wish I had a beautiful singing voice or
a great talent in sports or the arts. Father, help
me to find my gifts and to use them for Your
glory. And help me to remember that I am of
great value to You (Matthew 10:31).

Shame

When pride comes, then comes dishonor,
But with the humble is wisdom.
PROVERBS 11:2 NASB

*H*umility is hard to find in our society. In this age of selfies, we're full of ourselves. It's hard to be filled with the Holy Spirit when you're busy using a selfie stick to make sure you get the best shot. The angle has to be just right so that you look thin and attractive. Really, though, the very best angle we can hope to achieve is to see ourselves in a true light for the sinners we are. It's only by the grace of God that we are not destroyed.

God does not want us to walk around in shame. Jesus took our shame to the cross. Our sin was nailed to the cross and we bear it no more. But He does want us to walk in humility. If we are prideful, we will not gain the wisdom of our Lord. We are called to walk humbly with Him all of the days of our lives.

Help me never to be ashamed of You, Jesus. I know that one day when You come again, You will be ashamed of those who are ashamed of You (Luke 9:26).

I am so ashamed of my sin, Lord. It's always before me. Please remind me that when I ask You to forgive me, You are faithful to do so. I don't have to walk away hanging my head. I can stand tall. I am made righteous through my Savior's death on the cross for me. My sin is forgiven, and I can walk with confidence as a child of the living God.

You are the author and perfecter of my faith.
You took my shame upon Yourself and died
for me. You did not stay in the grave. You sit at
the right hand of God. You are my Savior and
Redeemer. You made a way for me to be a child
of God (Hebrews 12:2).

I'm ashamed to come before You. I am so sorry.
I can't even lift my face toward heaven. I have
not acted as a godly woman should. I've brought
disgrace to Your holy name. My iniquities have
risen above my head, and my guilt has grown
to the heavens (Ezra 9:6). And yet, I know that
when I lay my shame before You, You reach
down to me and embrace me. You call me Your
own. You're a good, good Father, and I am
loved by You.

Like Adam in the garden, attempting to hide his nakedness, I hide from You.

He heard the sound of You, Your spirit rustling through the trees.

I hear You, too. I hear the still, small voice of my Creator. . .but I block it out.

Hiding has become my norm.

I avoid prayer. I fill what used to be quiet times with the noise of life. I busy myself. I don't call it hiding. I call it work and school. I call it smartphone and tablet and social media. I call it caring for children, seeing to my husband's needs, and meeting deadlines at the office. I call it whatever I must so long as it can keep me from humbling myself before You.

I'm so ashamed of who I have become.

Oh God, in Your graciousness, peel back the layers of shame under which I have buried that part of me that walks and talks with You.

Look upon me with a Jesus lens, my sin covered by His lifeblood shed for me at Calvary.

It's the only way that I can show my face. He is the way, the truth, and the life. No one comes to the Father but through Him.

Toxic Friendships

Then Jonathan and David made a covenant,
because he loved him as his own soul.
1 Samuel 18:3 asv

Reading of Jonathan and David's friendship in the Bible is a great way to find an example of a healthy friendship. They were like brothers. They loved one another and looked out for one another's best interest.

When a friendship is one-sided, with one individual as the giver and the other only taking, something is terribly wrong. God does not want you to be manipulated or to be manipulative. He wants His children to have healthy, loving friendships in which they build one another up.

God never wants us to be involved in unhealthy relationships. He is not glorified through toxic friendships. Ask Him to show you how to find freedom from this toxic friendship that's tearing you down. You want to be yourself again, and it's not possible until you are free from this situation.

Heavenly Father, sometimes I feel like You want me to sacrifice myself to this friend. I feel like I should be a "good Christian" and just take the abuse. I know that's not a thought that comes from You. Help me to stand against Satan's schemes. You do not want your daughter to be treated poorly time and time again. Help me to know how to find freedom from this friendship that is so disheartening.

Jesus, this friend brings me down. After I spend time with her, I don't feel good about myself. She has a way of subtly knocking me down in order to build herself up. Give me words to speak so that I can convey my feelings to her. If she refuses to hear me, give me wisdom, Father, on whether to walk away from this friendship or attempt to continue it.

God, she's jealous. I see it in her eyes. I hear it in her snide comments. I don't know why she's so envious of my life. It's not like I have a perfect existence. I think she just sees certain ways You've blessed me and she wants these things for herself. She doesn't seem like a friend, Father. This seems more like an enemy. Help me to know how to handle this situation. How did I get so entrenched with someone who is not good for me?

God, You tell me in Your Word to guard my heart, for it is the wellspring of life. I didn't do that. I opened up to someone who wasn't safe. I wasn't sure at the time, but now I see that it was a big mistake. She has not been a faithful friend. She's shared things I told her in confidence and she's gossiped about me. It's so hard to know what to do. Show me whether to confront her or not, I pray. Give me a forgiving spirit toward this person, but give me wisdom so that I will not place trust in unsafe people again.

Lord, will You provide a new friendship for me? Will You place on my path a friend who will not do all the taking and all the talking? I need someone to listen to me sometimes, to care about my problems, to help me. I am tired of being the giver 100 percent of the time.

Thank You, Lord, for Your faithful friendship. You never leave me. You are always there. Even when I have strayed, You are still there waiting when I come to my senses. I love You, Lord.

God, it seems like this friendship started out okay, but things have changed. Help me to accept that not all friendships last a lifetime. It may be time to walk away from this one.

Unforgiveness

And Jesus said, Father, forgive them;
for they know not what they do.
LUKE 23:34 ASV

It's not always easy to forgive. However, as Christians we must follow Christ's example. If He could forgive the people who were killing Him, we can certainly find a way to forgive those who hurt us!

Ultimately, when we can't forgive, we hurt ourselves more than anyone. Nursing a grudge damages our own hearts. It can even make us physically ill.

God wants to set us free from old grievances and harbored resentment. He will heal our wounded hearts and give us the strength to forgive. After all, He forgave us, didn't He?

Lord Jesus, if You could forgive the people who stripped You and drove nails through Your hands and feet, those who hung You up on the cross to die, then I know You can help me to forgive those who have offended or wronged me.

God, free me of resentment and self-righteousness. Take the two-by-four out of my own eye before I worry too much about the speck in someone else's! Make me humble enough to forgive.

Jesus, in the Gospels, You always showed mercy to the sinners. But You had no patience for the proud and unforgiving Pharisees.

Lord, may I carry Your forgiveness to all who have hurt me. May they see You in me. Work Your reconciliation through me.

God, I know You want me to live at peace with others—but I won't be able to do that until I can forgive. Help me forgive that which seems unforgiveable. Free my heart so that I can be at peace with everyone.

Weakness

But those who trust in the LORD will find new strength.
They will soar high on wings like eagles. They will run
and not grow weary. They will walk and not faint.
ISAIAH 40:31 NLT

*H*ave you been to the gym lately? While you're
sweating away a mile or two on the treadmill,
have you glanced at the bodybuilders who are
lifting tremendous weights? Sometimes it's hard
not to stare! Their strength is amazing! The
muscles of their arms are bulging and defined.
They are focused, and—above all—they've
conditioned themselves day after day in order to
be strong enough to lift such weight.

God is stronger than any bodybuilder. He
is powerful enough to speak the world into
existence. He parted a sea and allowed His
people to walk through on dry land and then
brought the waters crashing down upon their
enemies. His touch can cause the blind to see
and the deaf to hear. In your weakness, He is
strong.

Lord, You see my weaknesses. You know the areas where I struggle. But I can do all things through You who gives me strength (Philippians 4:13).

Heavenly Father, strengthen me, I pray. May my strength come from Your might (Ephesians 6:10).

I want to soar as the eagles. I watch them, God. They take flight and so gracefully soar above the earth. I want my spirit to be light and free again. I feel so powerless in this situation. I am weak, but You are strong. Be my strength today. I ask this in the strong name of Your Son, Jesus.

Today I pray that You will go before me. In every moment of weakness, I pray You will show up to provide supernatural strength. Where I am failing, bring success. Where I am losing my grip, take hold. Where I am discouraged, lift me up. I will trust in You.

Some trust in chariots or horses. I trust in the name of the Lord my God (Psalm 20:7). I choose to walk in the strength of my Savior. I choose to rest in my Redeemer. I choose to endure because of Emmanuel—God with us. God before me. God with me. God beside me.

Christ, shield me today
Against wounding
Christ with me, Christ before me,
Christ behind me,
Christ in me, Christ beneath me,
Christ above me,
Christ on my right, Christ on my left,
Christ when I lie down, Christ when I sit down,
Christ in the heart of everyone
who thinks of me,
Christ in the mouth of everyone
who speaks of me,
Christ in the eye that sees me,
Christ in the ear that hears me.
I arise today
Through the mighty strength
Of the Lord of creation.

PRAYER OF SAINT PATRICK

Worry

Don't worry about anything; instead, pray about everything.
Tell God what you need, and thank him for all he has done.
PHILIPPIANS 4:6 NLT

Women are worriers. We worry about the people in our lives—our children, our parents, our spouses, our friends. We worry about gaining weight and losing money. We worry about the future. But where does all of that worry get us? Nowhere.

The Bible says that each day has enough worry of its own. In other words, don't borrow trouble. Worries keep us from experiencing the abundant life God has given us. They also say to God that we don't trust Him.

Focus on transforming your worries into prayers. Each time a worry occurs, form the habit of lifting it up to God. As you offer your cares to Him, they will lose their power to trample out the peace of God in your life.

God, I give You my present and my future because I know You can handle them better than I ever could. You have shown up in my past and provided for my every need. You have filled my life with blessings. Help me to trust You with the unknown by banking on what I do know—You are a faithful God.

You are a big God. You are bigger than all the little things I worry about. You are bigger than Satan who tries to drag me down with anxiety and fear. I claim the name of Jesus, and I pray for power to fight against the spiritual forces that battle daily against Christians.

Lord, You are *Jehovah-Jireh* (the Lord will provide). You provided a ram for Abraham to sacrifice in place of his beloved son Isaac. You provided right at the moment that a sacrifice was needed. Thank You for the assurance that You will provide for my needs as well. I can trust You all of my life—in every stage, at every crossroads. I will trust in my Provider.

You are with me and You are for me. If God is for me, who can be against me? What will it matter if they are? No one is stronger than my God.

Lord, like a mother hen protecting her chicks, You protect Your children (Psalm 91:4). I have no reason to worry or fear. You are always with me, watching over me, and laying out the path before me one step at a time. You don't give me more than I can handle. You created me and You know me better than I even know myself. I trust You, God.

God, You showed up for Daniel in the lions' den. You have proven time and time again in my own life that You always come through for Your children. You know what we need and when we need it. This life is a journey, and it's a lesson in trust. Help me to be a scholar who learns the lessons early so that I am not worrying my years away.

I'm struggling under the weight of a burden You could carry with ease. The problem is You won't fight me for it. You tell me to cast my cares upon You. You ask me to trust You and to lean not on my own understanding. You tell me that Your ways are higher than my ways (Isaiah 55:8–9) and that You know the plans You have for me (Jeremiah 29:11). And yet, I struggle under the weight of worry. Help me, Father, not to just pay lip service to surrender but to truly surrender. I keep picking the worries back up. Help me to deposit them fully and forever at the foot of Your throne. You are strong enough and wise enough to handle all of my concerns.